To Mom
With love
Betty Christmas
1981

The Dream Come True

The Dream Come True
Great Houses of Los Angeles

BRENDAN GILL
photographs by **DERRY MOORE**
and with the assistance of Christopher Phillips

LIPPINCOTT & CROWELL, PUBLISHERS
NEW YORK

For John Calmann

This book was designed and produced by John Calmann and Cooper Ltd, London

ISBN: 0-690-01893-2
     0-690-01961-0 sp. ed.

LIBRARY OF CONGRESS CATALOG CARD NUMBER: 80-7881

Endpapers: Satellite pictures of Los Angeles, by courtesy of NASA

Frontispiece: 1. The Perkins house, Pasadena, by Richard J. Neutra

Contents

Introduction

My earliest glimpses of Los Angeles and its environs were gathered at second hand from the movie comedies of Charlie Chaplin, Buster Keaton, and Harold Lloyd. The time that I speak of was well over fifty years ago, when the city had only a few hundred thousand inhabitants; now it has almost three million, making it the largest city in the country after New York and Chicago. (A more significant fact is that Los Angeles County, of which the city of Los Angeles is the seat, has a population of over seven million people and is the steadily expanding heart of the richest and most populous state in the union.) The buildings that one caught sight of in the background of those early movies formed a modest enough profile against the horizon. Here and there in the downtown business district a scattering of office-buildings rose to a height of eight or ten stories – it was from one of them that Harold Lloyd dangled in "Safety Last," clutching a clock-face that threatened to give way at any second – but for the most part the city hugged the ground on which it was built.

From the beginning, Los Angeles was settled by people whose dream was to acquire land of their own, houses of their own. Sharing that dream, succeeding waves of newcomers created a horizontal city – one that to this day is said to contain more private houses per capita than any other large city on earth. Generation after generation, the dream of ownership came true and continues to come true. For that reason, the city we see today and the city I saw in the movies of my childhood have more in common than one might expect. The differences are many, but so are the likenesses. The thinly sprawling Los Angeles of the twenties was made up of block after block of cheaply built low shop-fronts, clusters of fading turn-of-the-century Queen Anne houses, some big new mansions in concrete and stucco, and – more important than any other kind of structure – a great sea of pillared and latticed bungalows, stretching along the boulevards and trickling out as they approached the city's semi-circle of guardian foothills. The cheap shop-fronts and the Queen Anne houses have grown rare, but the mansions remain and are cherished (Muhammed Ali lives in one of the grandest of them), and behind the glittering scrim of the high-rises that line the boulevards the bungalows in their thousands and tens of thousands preserve seemingly unchanged the intentions of that other, more modest time. The boulevards of L.A. are assuredly hard-hitting Big Business – are we in Bogota? Singapore? Düsseldorf? What language is one expected to speak among these glassy monoliths? – but on the somnolent side-streets we discover that the city consists as before of private houses large and small and of people devoted (perhaps more confidently here than anywhere else in the country) to a self-delighting hedonism: they are having a good time under the sun.

So accustomed are we to the high-flown nomenclature of Los Angeles that we tend to accept without demur that exotic word "boulevard"; still, it may be worth pausing over for a moment, to weigh its meanings. Sunset Boulevard, Hollywood Boulevard, Wilshire Boulevard – the degree to which these names have woven themselves into the fabric of American life makes it hard for us to

2. In the eighties and nineties, American architects believed in heaping up ornament in the greatest possible profusion. This house on Bonnie Brae Street, in an old quarter of Los Angeles, threatens to explode out of sheer high spirits. Note the dainty pillar that helps to support the third-story balcony; it appears to have drifted in from another civilization altogether. The house might well have been designed not by an architect but by a calligrapher.

realize that "boulevard" was once little more than a semantic trap set by real-estate promoters who had a formidable number of empty lots to sell. Like the somewhat less impressive "avenue," "boulevard" comes from the French, and to our ancestors it hinted at the suave grandeur of Paris, paved and illuminated and echoing to the tunes of Offenbach. Far more than the commonplace English "street" and "road," it extended a promise of urban refinement to the emerging middle class, which was largely rural in origin and romantic in its aspirations. Throughout the United States in the nineteenth and early twentieth centuries, many so-called boulevards sprang into instant existence in newspaper advertisements and were subsequently found to be but dusty wagon-trails winding through swamps and deserts.

It was, for example, characteristic of Eastern real-estate speculators that in the rocky wasteland of the Bronx – known as the bedroom of New York City – they platted and sold lots facing upon something called the Grand Boulevard and Concourse, not the least of whose distinctions was that it possessed exactly the same width as the Champs Elysées. Similarly, it was characteristic of real-estate speculators in the West that Wilshire Boulevard should have been named after the engaging rascal who helped to develop it – H. Gaylord Wilshire, who made and lost many fortunes in the course of a bizarre and happy life and who died defending the utility of an electric belt of his invention, guaranteed to cure arthritis, heart disease, diabetes, paralysis, and cancer. As thoughts of the Champs Elysées softened the harshness of the Bronx, so every syllable of Wilshire's name bespoke aristocratic origins and vouched for the value of the sorry-looking land he peddled. Much of Wilshire Boulevard was, in Spanish days, *El Camino Real*, or the King's Highway, but almost within living memory there were long stretches of it that were mere idle small-town sand and brush.

3. The cowboy actor and newspaper columnist Will Rogers lived on this ranch on Sunset Boulevard in Pacific Palisades. It is now a state park bearing his name and containing among other artifacts the wooden horse on which he used to practice playing polo. When Rogers became the first honorary Mayor of Beverly Hills, he announced in his inaugural address, "It is my intention to elevate motion-picture folk and real-estate men to the level of the common people."

4. The grandly continental entrance gates to Pickfair, long the home of Mary Pickford and Douglas Fairbanks. The estate belies its origin as a ramshackle shooting-box in the scrub woods high above the hundreds of acres of bean-fields that were one day to become Beverly Hills.

5. (Overleaf left) Two brothers – Charles Sumner Greene and Henry Mather Greene – were for long among the leading architects in the Los Angeles area. Their houses give the impression of being primordially cave-like; under the shelter of those broad roofs, one feels safe from any ancient danger. This is the Blacker house, in Pasadena, built in 1912. The front door is of Tiffany glass and the cat might well be a thousand years old.

6. (Overleaf right) A. Quincy Jones was an architect who, not fearing to be damned as "eclectic", moved gracefully through a variety of styles, taking care to embody in the design of houses the aesthetic intentions of his clients as well as his own. This house in Pasadena, built in the 1970s, is self-confidently *à la mode*. What appear at first glance to be certain pieces of sculpture against the glass doors at the rear of the room are, in fact, a hat-rack and an umbrella stand.

Playing over in memory those jumpy, silent comedies of long ago, we encounter scores of clues as to how Los Angeles developed, not only out of sand and brush but out of wheatfields, orchards, and orange and lemon groves as well. (A farmer abandoning the Middle West for Southern California dreamed not of giving up farming but of farming in his shirt-sleeves, under a blue sky, in a climate without winters.) A movie chase might begin on foot, but it nearly always employed automobiles and trolley-cars to heighten the dangers faced by a beleaguered hero. In land area and in population, Los Angeles kept doubling in size from one decade to the next, and an efficient system of inter-urban rapid-transit played a large part in making this growth possible. As the old land-grants of Spanish Colonial times were sold and broken up into sub-divisions, the big red trolley-cars of the Pacific Electric Railway provided the transportation that linked new communities to one another and to a still dominant downtown Los Angeles. These trolley-cars, which went careering along their own rights-of-way or along the middle strips of boulevards, often at speeds of up to sixty miles an hour, were among the first props that the infant movie industry chose to take advantage of when it settled in Hollywood. What movie can it have been in which I recall a hero of mine clinging to a trolley-pole on the roof of a P.E. car as it swung perilously round a bend in the tracks? Or saw him leaping nimbly from the roof of a trolley-car traveling at high speed in one direction to the roof of a trolley-car traveling at an equally high speed in the opposite direction, thus permitting him to outwit his villainous pursuers, who – such are the benefits of memory – will go on angrily shaking their fists at him forever?

A movie historian specializing in the period might well claim that *all* of Los Angeles amounted in those days to a single gorgeous prop for movies – a sort of open-air warehouse filled with an incomparable variety of settings, both natural and manufactured. The scoundrelly founders of the industry had abandoned their improvised studios in New York and New Jersey partly in order to avoid litigation with Thomas A. Edison, whose patents they were infringing, and partly in order to seek the sun, abundant and dependable light being the first requirement of the then primitive technology of movie-making. (Keaton told me once that he had begun his career in the movies in a converted livery stable on the East Side of Manhattan. A certain number of skylit studios had been fitted into the structure, but on rainy days shooting had to be suspended, and for this the actors were grateful: dampness brought out the latent odor of half a century of ghostly urine and manure. Keaton took readily to the fresh air of Southern California.) The industry built its studios in Hollywood – ironically, a town established some years earlier by a prim Prohibitionist couple from Topeka, who would have regarded movies as a form of moral leprosy. Within a few years, Hollywood was a name famous throughout the world not for propriety and abstemiousness but for wine, women, and song. It became an epitome of sexual licence, and from time to time a lovers' quarrel ending in murder or a lonely, drug-induced suicide reenforced its reputation as a contemporary Sodom. The Mrs Grundys of the world rejoiced to shake their heads and purse their lips over the extravagance and depravity of movie stars, and "to go Hollywood" became an accepted

verb, meaning roughly to turn one's success into an occasion for showing off, with a scandalous want of decorum.

The movies brought wealth to Los Angeles, but the lives that movie stars led, or were reputed to lead, were as remote from the lives of their fellow-citizens as they were from the lives of people living in Pittsburgh or Bangor. Hollywood was called a dream factory and the dreams it manufactured were for the whole world and not merely for Southern Californians. With increasing prosperity, actors, producers, directors, screen-writers, designers, and other beneficiaries of movie money and movie fame chose to live not in Hollywood itself but in the adjacent community of Beverly Hills, a city of just under six square miles existing within the boundaries of Los Angeles County but totally independent of it. Beverly Hills was – and is – as pretty and artificial as if it had been made out of spun sugar. It has no hospitals, because nobody is ever supposed to be sick there. It has no cemeteries, because nobody is ever supposed to die there. The building in Beverly Hills for which people feel the most reverence is not a church but a hotel; with a simplicity that kings might envy, it is called the Beverly Hills Hotel. An artificial gas-fire burns in a fireplace in the lobby all the year round; one is tempted to genuflect before it, as before an altar, on one's way into the Polo Lounge for lunch and the usual reconnoiterings and obeisances. ("George, how are you? Have you heard from Katie?")

The history of Beverly Hills amounts to a capsule history of the entire Los Angeles area. It is a movie scenario in which a once semi-arid countryside, having drudged through years of repeated failure, is able to achieve an ending that most of the people there appear to regard as both happy and everlasting. (Movie scenarios leave out the black slum of Watts and the *chicano* barrio of East Los Angeles, along with other blemishes.) In aboriginal times, the land was occupied by a few thousand notably unambitious Indians, who hunted and fished and never troubled to learn the art of farming. In 1769, a small colonizing expedition of monks and soldiers journeyed up out of Mexico and with trinkets and tobacco "purchased" in the name of the King of Spain some twelve thousand square miles of Indian territory. In 1781, a mission and village were founded near the banks of a river that the Spanish called El Rio de Nuestra Señora La Reina de los Angeles de Porciuncula. (The monks in the expedition were members of the Order of St Francis and Porciuncula was the name of a church that St Francis was known to have worshipped in.) By the end of a couple of decades, the mission and village of Los Angeles were securely established, but much of the Indian population had been wiped out, either by diseases that the white man had introduced or by overwork and despair, for as laborers the Indians were an expendable commodity, herded together for mass baptisms, ruthlessly exploited, and then dispatched to God.

The first house in what is now Beverly Hills was built by a woman named Maria Vita Valdez, a grand-daughter of one of the guides who had accompanied the expedition of 1769. Of the usual adobe construction, the house was put up in the early eighteen-thirties and stood near the present juncture of Sunset Boulevard and Alpine Drive, in the midst of a ranch that

7. One sees in the Blacker house how deftly the Greene brothers borrowed Oriental motifs, not so much in order to strike a note of delicacy as to strike a note of strength. Even so trifling a domestic necessity as a downspout is fashioned as if to last for centuries and so acquires an unexpected dignity.

covered well over four thousand acres. The property bore the romantic-sounding name of El Rancho Rodeo de las Aguas, or the Ranch of the Gathering of the Waters, denoting the fact that several streams came down out of the foothills and mingled in a canyon there. Having been long in possession of the ranch, in 1841 Doña Maria sought and obtained an official land-grant from the Mexican government. Five years later, Mexico and the United States were at war. Doña Maria fled from the approaching Yankee soldiers, who captured the village of Los Angeles without a skirmish and who then proceeded to loot the outlying ranches. The Valdez house was broken into and a trunk containing the land-grant documents was carried away, never to be recovered. By 1848, the United States had won the war and — what had always

14

8. In California, the vogue for what is currently known as "high-tech" – short for "high technology" – goes back at least as far as Neutra in the thirties; elsewhere in the world, it can be found in the work of such nineteenth-century architects as Labrouste in Paris and Stanford White in New York. Architects first thought of using industrial components as a way of saving money, but this has generally proved an illusion; what high-tech achieves is a sort of airy openness, coupled with surprise.

9. (Right) In the house of Diane and Harry Abramson, the apotheosis of the conversation pit. From its carpeted depths, one looks out across the living-room, through a dining-room approximately eighteen feet wide and a hundred feet long, to a green lawn and a prospect of distant hills. The Abramsons have permitted themselves the mild eccentricity of possessing neither a tennis court nor a swimming pool.

10. The classic Los Angeles house is a one-story-high bungalow, set on a narrow lot with a neat patch of green lawn in front and in back. Though diminutive in scale, the bungalow is often touchingly grand in aspiration – a doll's house version of a pillared state capitol building or a Palladian governor's mansion. In the parts of the city where such bungalows flourish, there are always sidewalks, and contrary to the rumor that nobody in Los Angeles ever walks – that walking is regarded, indeed, as a sign of possible criminal activity – many people, young and old, are to be seen on these sidewalks, strolling, roller-skating, or pushing baby-carriages.

been its intention – had fulfilled the nation's "manifest destiny" by acquiring California. In 1851, a U.S. Board of Commissioners was set up to examine the validity of the innumerable land-grants that had been issued over many generations by the Spanish and Mexican governments. The Valdez grant was upheld and Doña Maria had her property restored to her, but by then, being elderly, she appears to have found the management of the ranch too much for her. She sold it to a pair of land-developers, Major Henry Hancock and B. D. Wilson, for something like three thousand dollars, of which only five hundred dollars was in cash.

One might assume that anyone able, in the eighteen-fifties, to purchase four thousand acres of the fairest land in Southern California would soon make an immense fortune out of it, but nothing of the kind: Hancock and Wilson (who were later to make a great deal of money from other real-estate speculations in and around Los Angeles) tried raising wheat on the ranch, without success. The most severe drought in history set in and lasted the better part of a decade; crops failed and cattle died by the thousands. A tiny boom in oil – oil being used as fuel for lamps in those days and not for heating and transportation – got under way in the eighteen-sixties and quickly petered out. By 1870, the Ranch of the Gathering of the Waters had been sold several times over, on one occasion to a group of German immigrants, who laid out on paper a town to be called Santa Maria. The town having attracted no settlers, the ranch was sold to a couple of local farmers named Hammel and Denker, who planted it to beans. In the eighteen-eighties, Los Angeles and nearby Santa Monica enjoyed a brief, frenzied building boom. The Southern Pacific Railroad ran trains daily between the two communities, over a right-of-way that passed through the heart of the ranch. Real-estate speculators arranged for a train station to be built at what is now Canon Drive, with the intention of founding a town, Morocco, that would occupy approximately the same area as the earlier, ill-fated Santa Maria. Morocco never got beyond being a fancy drawing on the speculators' office-wall.

In 1906, the Hammel and Denker ranch was sold to a newly formed organization called the Rodeo Land and Water Company, for a price of just under seven hundred thousand dollars. The man who headed the organization, Burton Green, was a director of the Amalgamated Oil Company, which had sought in vain to locate oil in commercially worthwhile amounts on the property. If money could not be made from oil, Green reasoned that perhaps it could be made from real estate, despite so many failed attempts in the past, and not by the usual hit-or-miss development of an ordinary subdivision but by the founding of a town designed as a whole and down to the smallest details according to strict aesthetic and economic standards – a town that would be the embodiment of the increasingly sophisticated dreams of an increasingly wealthy middle class. To this end, Green called on a New York City landscape architect named Wilbur Cook to lay out a model town, with broad, gently curving roads that rose with the gradual slope of the land to the point where the chunky, almost untraversible foothills began. Green was an Easterner, and for the name of his new town he borrowed a portion of the name of his birthplace – Beverly Farms, Massachusetts. The town was incorporated in

18

1914, with a population of five hundred and fifty people – a narrow squeak, since for the privilege of incorporation a minimum of five hundred inhabitants was required.

That the town prospered was thanks to the arrival of the so-called "movie people" from adjacent Hollywood. The first of them was Douglas Fairbanks, a handsome and extremely popular actor-acrobat, who in 1919 purchased, for thirty-five thousand dollars, and remodeled, a hunting lodge on a large tract of land on Summit Drive – the highest point in town. At the time, Fairbanks was in love with Mary Pickford, the most famous movie star of the day. Known as "America's Sweetheart", she had blue eyes and long, golden curls, and she conveyed in movies an air of virginal purity that was often threatened but never violated. In Pickford's private life, matters were somewhat more complicated. She and Fairbanks were both married at the time that they fell in love and two difficult divorce-actions had to be got through before they were free to become man and wife. Once they had moved into 1141 Summit Drive, which the press rather than its owners immediately christened Pickfair, they became the leaders of local society, such as it was. The house and grounds grew grander with the years and so did the ambition of the Fairbankses; like royalty, they took care to entertain only the most distinguished visitors to Hollywood, and as a consequence an invitation to Pickfair was as avidly sought after as a private audience with the Pope. The Fairbankses were Anglophiles (Fairbanks was eventually to marry a Lady Ashley), and it was natural that when Lord and Lady Mountbatten arrived in Hollywood on their honeymoon they were put up in the guest-wing at Pickfair. By that time, Charlie Chaplin

11. It is true of houses as of people that, having fallen upon hard times, they strive to preserve a certain dignity. This house has literally gone into trade, but its gable gallantly pretends not to notice what is happening on the ground floor.

12. (Right) At the turn of the century, Los Angeles and its cluster of satellite communities were linked by an admirable system of trains and inter-urban trolley-cars. This crossing, on the way to Pasadena, would have been a commonplace then; now it is a rarity, precious to railroad buffs.

was a next-door neighbor and close friend of the Fairbankses, as well as a British citizen, and the Mountbattens, the Fairbankses, and Chaplin had a jolly time making an impromptu "home" movie together.

Will Rogers, a celebrated vaudevillian and newspaper columnist, was elected the first Mayor of Beverly Hills. As the owner of much real estate there and in nearby communities, he was far from shy about singing the praises of Beverly Hills in his syndicated column; at his death, his various real-estate

13, 14. (Left and above) For lack of any better term, Americans borrowed the word "Victorian" from England, to describe almost any structure built between the crowning of Victoria, in 1837, and her death, in 1901. From about 1920 to 1950, "Victorian" commonly served as a term of abuse in America, whether in regard to art, decoration, or architecture. Tens of thousands of houses like these were torn down during that period. Now they are cherished; as much as half a million dollars will be spent on a ruinous house that cost only five thousand dollars to build.

holdings were found to be worth many millions of dollars. If Beverly Hills flourished, so did its neighbors: among them Bel Air, Brentwood, and Pacific Palisades. It is a notion widely accepted in American life that "old" money is somehow better than "new", and in Los Angeles in the twenties and thirties Bel Air attracted the attention of old money, as Pasadena had done half a century earlier. Prosperous Middle Westerners built winter homes for themselves in a climate welcomely unlike the blizzardy, sub-zero climate of the Great Lakes and the Great Plains, and Easterners of wealth and comparatively ancient lineage found increasing reason to prefer California to the aggressive banalities of the resort cities of Florida. Not only climate drew strangers to the farthest of our shores; politics, which in times of trouble can become a matter literally of life and death, also played a part: in the forties, many refugees of international reputation – Thomas Mann, Arnold Schönberg, Lion Feuchtwanger, and the like – settled in Pacific Palisades, making it for a few years a sort of intellectual and artistic outpost of the Europe that Hitler had forced them to abandon. Southern California has long been notorious as the breeding-ground for radically eccentric political and religious cults; the freedom that permits such cults to flourish permits a host of eccentric individuals – writers, artists, architects, philosophers – to experiment unobserved and underided with a variety of unpopular modes of expression and conduct.

Before the Second World War, shipping, the oil industry, and the movie industry (surely the only new art form in history that from its beginnings insisted upon being known as an industry) were the chief sources of wealth for the sprawling conurbation of "L.A."; after the war, what was to become known as the aero-space industry usurped this role and mightily expanded it. In the train of aero-space came more and more banks, insurance companies, savings-and-loan associations, and other liege-lords and vassals of big money. Characteristically, the so-called Miracle Mile on Wilshire Boulevard – the High Holy Place of the Consumer God – has been turned into mile after mile of recurrent miracles, with blanched, domino-like office buildings leaping skyward as if on Michigan Boulevard, in Chicago, or on the Avenue of the Americas, in New York. What are they doing there, these impertinent high-rises, in a city so prodigal of land that tens of thousands of its houses are but one story high and a single parking lot will extend over many acres? No explanation will serve save pride: a great city must make a great show in the world. The small-town feeling of the Los Angeles of Will Rogers survives and prospers under a variety of disguises, but the city as a whole has been transformed in purpose as well as in scale. It is a city of hedonists, their faces to the sun; it is also a city of millions of workers, whose energy is as unmistakable and as unremitting as the night-and-day hum of cars on the 800-odd miles of freeways – those elegant earthworks that, like the old, rosy city-wall round Lucca, happen to combine beauty and utility. Lying in bed, one listens to that hum and thinks not of the lost silences of an earlier day but of the fact that it is the mark of a great city never to sleep. In its zestful ambitions for itself, Los Angeles is the second city of the country. Few doubt that it stands ready to be the first.

22

By an irony, a city that cultivates an air of constantly renewed novelty is among the oldest in the country. In 1981, Los Angeles will be celebrating the two hundredth anniversary of its founding. Its age is all the more remarkable because from the start it has existed in defiance of nature. The first of its needs was water. In the eighteenth century, the little Los Angeles River provided the struggling pueblo with a sufficient supply for domestic purposes, as well as for the irrigation of fields and orchards. The climate of the region is Mediterranean – real-estate boosters used to describe Southern California as "the land of eternal springtime" – and although rain is an occasion for apology in Los Angeles between April and November, the soil has only to be properly watered to bloom and bear in a continuous, improbable commingling of blossoms and fruits. Having come from a semi-arid homeland, where for centuries a knowledge of the science of hydraulics was a necessary commonplace, the Spanish explorers, in the course of setting up missions, villages, and military posts along the Pacific coast, taught the native Indians much about the damming of streams, the digging of ditches, the tapping of underground watercourses, and the building of aqueducts. In the nineteenth century, as the city, seesawing constantly between boom and bust, shook itself free of the confinement of the old pueblo, it was assumed that it would fail to become a major metropolis because of the scarcity of available water.

At the turn of the twentieth century, William Mulholland, the gifted engineer who presided over the development of the Los Angeles water system, predicted that the city could expect never to sustain a population of more than two hundred thousand people, unless . . . This crafty, admonitory "unless" proved to embrace the floating of several municipal bond issues, making it possible for the city to draw water all the way from the Owens River Valley, some two hundred and fifty miles to the north, in the High Sierra. The project, begun in 1907, was completed in 1913. "Take it!" Mulholland said, as the first Owens River Valley water started flowing into the city's pipes, and the city eagerly did so, for the new system was capable of supplying four times as much water as the city consumed. Mulholland became a local hero, perhaps in part because he refused to capitalize politically upon his fame. "I would rather give birth to a porcupine backwards," he said, "than be the Mayor of Los Angeles."

Despite Mulholland's exceptional preference, politics and water have been closely linked in the history of cities, above all in localities where water is naturally in short supply. The extra water available from the Owens River Valley system was certain not to go to waste – on the contrary, the system may well have been designed from the beginning to benefit a number of private individuals whose interest lay less in bringing water to Los Angeles than in bringing it to the nearby San Fernando Valley. That vast, level, and fertile region had only to be irrigated in order to become an agricultural Garden of Eden. Knowing this, a handful of prominent figures in town formed a syndicate to buy at a cheap price something like fifty thousand acres of farmland in the Valley; with the addition of water, a profit of tens of millions of dollars would be easily realized. By Federal regulation (for President Theodore Roosevelt appears to have smelled a rat in the enabling legislation

15. A house out of the Gay Nineties, which even in California were perhaps less gay than they were later reported to have been. Here is a portion of a big wooden house in what is known in America as the Queen Anne style, in part because nobody in America then knew anything about Queen Anne. What the term signified was an open floor-plan, high gables, a front piazza, and a round tower springing up at one side of the structure, accompanied by a rich encrusting of carved ornament.

and court decisions by which the Owens River Valley had been snatched from its original owners), the water from the Valley was to go only to the citizens of Los Angeles. Politicians had no difficulty in outwitting that seemingly iron-clad stipulation: the city voted to annex the San Fernando Valley, and the boom was on. The device of annexation proved so attractive in its simplicity that it was resorted to again and again. Water for the people was the lure, the motive a secret profit of millions for a few light-fingered insiders. As a consequence, the physical size of Los Angeles quadrupled between 1913 and 1923. (Beverly Hills, Culver City, and Santa Monica chose to remain independent cities, entirely surrounded by the city of Los Angeles.) There have been a few additions in recent years, the latest scraps of hill and dale having been gathered up in 1977. The city now embraces a total of four hundred and sixty-four square miles – by comparison, the land area of New York City amounts to only three hundred and twenty square miles – and no further annexations are said to be in prospect.

Cupidity isn't necessarily the worst of motives in the development of a great city; one could argue, indeed, that it is an indispensable one. Whatever the scheming that may have lain behind the Owens River Valley project, the fact is

that Los Angeles continues to enjoy an ample supply of water in its desert-like setting, as hundreds of thousands of constantly besprinkled patches of bright-green lawn and garden attest through the long dry summers. Since Mulholland's day, the water system has tapped the resources of the Mono Basin and the Colorado River, both hundreds of miles distant from the city – feats of hydraulic engineering so far-sighted that it will probably be many years before Los Angeles needs to draw from the Colorado the full amount of water to which it is entitled by Federal and inter-state agreements.

Abundant water, abundant land – for with the extension of freeways into open country, the amount of real estate available appears to increase even as it is being used up – and a climate as nearly perfect as any in the country, with the advantage, in terms of recreation, of miles of readily accessible beach, forest, mountain, and desert: no wonder that the population of Los Angeles continues to rise! Who are these latter-day settlers? Are their aspirations any different from those of the settlers who arrived by train in the building boom of a hundred years ago? Or from those of the settlers of fifty years ago, arriving by car and truck and trailer, many of them among the first victims of a deepening Great Depression? As far as one can judge, the present newcomers seek what newcomers to Los Angeles have always sought: to better their fates, to make themselves more nearly their own masters, to be rooted at last in their own soil. And they have come by whatever reckoning to the right place, because Los Angeles, celebrated throughout the world for its wealth and conspicuous display, is also, though at first glance almost invisibly, a city in which quite modest dreams can come true. The houses currently being offered for sale at two or three million dollars (even proud Pickfair has been put on the market, at an asking price of twelve million dollars) are certainly characteristic of Los Angeles; no less characteristic is an anonymous bungalow on a side-street off less fashionable Melrose Avenue, offered for sale at eighty thousand dollars.

Contrary to what a casual visitor might suppose, Los Angeles is an agreeably humble city. It is at peace with its flimsiness; much of it could vanish overnight in a high wind and be rebuilt within a week or two. The climate invites impromptu construction, just as it invites impromptu living. Few architects took part in the building booms of earlier days; tens of thousands of houses that have survived admirably into the present were put up by a builder who happened to see a pretty picture in a magazine, sometimes accompanied by floor-plans and sometimes not. That was the house he chose to build, and not once but again and again, content with what would sell. Such a house sat on its own narrow plot of land, with small yards at front and back, and every room in the house had at least one window, including the kitchen and the bathroom. Cross-ventilation and an open gabled attic helped keep the house cool in summer without air-conditioning, as did awnings at the windows and a low-roofed verandah that, hung with plants, turned the entrance into a bowery grotto. Filling block after block, street after street, these cookie-cutter houses continue to make up a sizeable portion of Los Angeles, and very satisfactory dwellings they are, though they will gain but a curt footnote in architectural history: "vernacular" is the kindest word that is likely to be applied to them.

17. An Art Deco sunburst window.

16. (Left) One might expect to encounter this statue of the crucified Christ by a roadside high in the Austrian Alps; instead, here it is in Southern California, serving to temper the sun on a pleasant terrace overlooking the sea. Curiously, the statue appears at home in this setting, perhaps because Spanish monks were carrying the cross up the Pacific coast two centuries ago, founding missions and converting the local Indians.

18. The Beverly Hills Hotel was originally designed in what is loosely known as the Mission style. It occupies a prominent site on Sunset Boulevard and has been continuously fashionable since it opened in 1912. In the early days, patrons of the hotel were not much given to swimming or tennis, much less to sun-bathing, and they spent much of their time rocking back and forth on the ample front verandah of the hotel. The verandah was long ago rendered obsolete by additions to the fabric of the hotel and is used today mostly for the storage of luggage dollies. A gas fire roars winter and summer on the hearth in the lobby; meanwhile, most of the activity is taking place either in the Polo Lounge or out by the swimming pool. Not to be seen using a telephone by the poolside is a sign of humiliating entrepreneurial failure.

Distinguished architecture is nearly always a product of the expenditure of large sums of money, which is by no means the same as saying that the expenditure of large sums of money produces distinguished architecture. It is only to say that gifted architects are likely to be more expensive than hacks, which is as it should be. I. M. Pei observed to me once that if a building proves to be an aesthetic success, forty per cent of the credit should go to the client. The percentage struck me as high, but Pei was vehement on the point, and who should know better than he? In the case of the design for the East Building of the National Gallery of Art, in Washington, D.C., the client, Paul Mellon, permitted Pei to spend something over a hundred million dollars on a building that could easily have been built on a lesser scale, with less refinement of workmanship, for perhaps eighty million dollars. The twenty-million-dollar difference sets a great patron apart from any ordinary one.

For many generations now, distinguished architects have practiced in Los Angeles, and perhaps it has been the lack of great patrons that has caused their handiwork to be so little regarded by the world at large. True, the city has no superb domestic follies on the order of the Pulitzer house in New York, the Hill house in St Paul, the Oelrichs house in Newport. Houses of an equivalent cost have been designed, in most cases, by mediocre architects for rock stars and other ephemeral entertainers; catching sight of their twenty-foot-high front doors and tiny mansard roofs, we shake our heads in wonder but not in admiration. Marcus Aurelius said that even in a palace life can be lived well. That is to take the palace as seriously as we take its occupants: it must be lofty in intention as well as in construction. Moreover, the distinguished architects I speak of have often been obliged to work for clients of limited means – people who, far from supplying the twenty-million-dollar difference, have been hard-pressed to supply a thousand-dollar one. Especially in hard times, these architects have found themselves designing houses not for a Maecenas but, often enough, for a school-teacher, and the relative costliness of their services has been demonstrated on an infinitesimal scale.

Hitherto, I have been dealing mainly with the anonymous architecture of Los Angeles; I turn now to the work of a handful of individual architects. For though a type of house – an eighteenth-century Colonial salt-box, say – can be loosely called great, as being representative of a certain style of high merit, if a single house deserves to be called great, it is because it is great in an inimitable way; the benign ghost of its designer will be hovering in every nook and cranny. Among the architects at work in Los Angeles in succeeding decades of the twentieth century have been the Greene brothers, Frank Lloyd Wright, his son Lloyd Wright, Irving Gill, Reginald Johnson, Wallace Neff, R. M. Schindler, Richard Neutra, Thornton M. Abell, A. Quincy Jones, Craig Ellwood, and Cliff May. How skeptically would such a group dine together in some architectural elysium and how little, in most cases, would they have to say to one another, except in bibulous disputation!

Charles Sumner Greene (1868–1957) and Henry Mather Greene (1870–1954) were born in the Middle West and journeyed east to receive their architectural training at the Massachusetts Institute of Technology, from which they were graduated in 1892. It would be hard to exaggerate the variety of influences to which the young Greenes were subject at that time. The formidable H. H. Richardson, dead since 1886, remained a powerful figure, not least because two of his favorite draftsmen, Charles Follet McKim and Stanford White, were founding partners in the most fashionable architectural firm in the country – McKim, Mead & White. Earlier, McKim and White had been champions of shingle, timber, and stone, in the virile style of their master. Their unassuming casino in Newport had been a new thing in the world, simultaneously Richardsonian and Japanese; now the firm was moving back into history, adapting Renaissance models to American needs. Elsewhere, the style of the so-called craftsman movement, descended from William Morris, collided not unfruitfully with the Mission style, named, however inaccurately, for the Spanish missions of the American Southwest. Neo-Colonial had its enthusiasts and so did the emerging Chicago School. Never in America had there been so rich a mingling of architectural possibilities, and the mingling was never to be so rich again, for little by little as the years passed aesthetic preferences hardened and narrowed into convictions. To make matters more difficult, critics of architecture began to place a heavier intellectual burden upon the architect than he had been accustomed to carry: no longer was he to be a sort of magpie, free to make a nest out of whatever materials struck his or a client's fancy – running up a Hawaiian bungalow for someone on Monday and an Anne Hathaway cottage for someone else on Tuesday. Like writers and artists, he was to buckle down and confront his unconscious, conveying to us through his work what he thought he saw there. He and his work were to be indissolubly one.

By 1894, the Greenes had moved west and set up practice in Pasadena, an already flourishing community. It took the brothers some years to develop a style that would express their view of how they and other people should be content to live: simply and unaggressively within the conventional bounds of conduct and without material clutter, among objects that took their beauty from nature. The hand-made was already in vogue, especially in Southern California; a prosperous middle class, though grateful to be the beneficiary of the Industrial Revolution, was eager to express its personal sensitivity through a counter-revolution espousing arts and crafts. Products of the machine-age (stoves, furnaces, toilets) were a necessary evil, to be kept as far out of sight as possible. The Greenes gave this vogue an authentically artistic form. Their houses celebrate wood with a primordial fervor; coming upon a Greene and Greene house, with its shaggy pelt of split-shake cedar shingles, its boldly exposed rafters and beams, one imagines that a portion of some distant forest has been carried to the site and imperfectly domesticated in order to provide shelter for a human family, but that the energy of its forest nature continues to flow. The house is at rest on its site and yet doesn't pretend that it has always belonged there. An accommodation has had to be made between it and the

20. (Right) Whether they were aware of it or not, the masons who carved the stonework of this house were following the centuries-old tradition of masons throughout all of Europe, who never lost an opportunity to pay their lords and masters the tribute of a likeness. One thinks of the carved visages smiling out upon the street from the house of Jacques Coeur, in Bourges, and regrets not being able to salute by name the couple who, surely for many decades to come, will go on bidding the world welcome from their secure perch above the front door.

19. (Left) In a well-policed enclave in an older section of Los Angeles, the rich of sixty or seventy years ago built themselves immense stucco mansions in the neo-Renaissance style. Henry James said once that, everything else being equal, a building that sits is more pleasing than a building that stands; this house, owned by Muhammed Ali, sits with an air of consummate self-satisfaction upon its broad, bright-green carpet of continuously besprinkled lawn.

surrounding landscape by means of terraces, lawns, and gardens – a further stage of domestication. At first glance, the house may put us in mind of Japan (where the Greenes never set foot); at a second glance, we are likely to think of those fierce ancient stave churches of the Norsemen, in which, when we place a hand on one of its timbers, we feel an uncanny surge of strength.

As early as the eighteen-sixties, in summer resorts along the New Jersey shore, architects were designing what were known as "hygienic" cottages for the new men on Wall Street, a short sea-journey away. By dint of cross-

21. A characteristic feature of much of the cityscape of Los Angeles is the alley, which provides a means of carrying out most of the grubby tasks of residential life – the garaging of cars, the delivery of groceries, the collection of garbage, the reading of gas and electric meters, and the like. It also serves on occasion as a sluiceway, carrying off with welcome speed (and cleaning itself in the process) the sudden, violent downpours of the short rainy season.

ventilation in every room and a three-story-high central hall, fresh air was drawn constantly into the house, up the funnel of the hall, and out through an open cupola on the roof. Forty years later, the Greene brothers practiced a similar but more subtle hygiene in Pasadena and Los Angeles. The so-called "billiard room" on the third floor of the Gamble house (which never held a billiard table – the Gambles didn't believe in billiards) and the seventy-foot-long gabled attic of the Blacker house, open at both ends, are highly effective devices for the moving of air. Wherever possible, they tried to match the orientation of a house to the direction of the prevailing winds; in the case of the Gamble house they were outwitted by Mrs Gamble, who, perhaps fearing the derision of neighbors, insisted that the house be located in the usual way, parallel to the street upon which it faces.

The Greenes' intentions in the designs they undertook are both circumspect and passionate. Circumspect, because it is plain from a study of the floor-plans of their houses that the ordinary daily lives of their bourgeois clients are not to be unduly spiritualized by exquisite surroundings; servants provide the usual creature comforts, going about their duties efficiently, and for the most part invisibly, by means of back-passages and back-stairs (in the Gamble house, sounds generated in the service area are kept from the living area by a system of double doors). What is passionate in their intentions can be observed in the detailing, which sometimes approaches the obsessional. The interior framing of a Greene and Greene house, of rich wood hand-rubbed to a mirror-like finish, is often more massive than it has any reason to be; sometimes a heavy wood member, reassuring to the eye, supports only itself. A front door several feet wide, into which a landscape of Tiffany glass has been set, will have smaller doors on either side. It is these smaller doors that are commonly in use, both as passageways and for ventilation; the middle door has been promoted to the status of an immovable work of art. Hinges, downspouts, electric lamps, the very outlets into which the lamps are plugged – all have been given importance through a rare combination of refinement and exaggeration. Plainly, the Greene brothers harbored powerful emotions and were less decorous in their hearts than the rather prim photographs taken of them in their prime would lead us to believe.

Between 1919 and 1923, an architect was intermittently at work in Los Angeles who was never circumspect and always passionate and who would have torn into shreds instantly any photograph of him that caused him to look prim. This architect was, of course, Frank Lloyd Wright. He was the greatest American architect of his time and he was always the first to say so; on most occasions, he would have omitted "American" and on some occasions he would have substituted "all" for "his". He sang his praises with charm and wit and, when he was taking what he called "a worm's eye-view of the world", with bitterness. Freud says that no man who has been his mother's favorite knows what it is to fear failure, and it was the case with Wright, who had indeed been his mother's favorite, that although he often suffered failure, he never feared it: sooner or later, his wrong-headed adversaries were bound to perceive that his way was the only correct one. He was a small, fine-boned man, with blue eyes and a skin so smooth that it appeared never to need shaving. His manner was gracefully imperious and his style of dress had a calculated touch of eccentricity. Not knowing him to be an architect, one might mistake him for an impresario or perhaps a magician – there would be no reason for surprise if, with a snap of his fingers, he commanded a dozen white doves to emerge from the top of his broad-brimmed, pork-pie hat.

When Miss Aline Barnsdall, a resident of Los Angeles, asked Wright to design a building for her there, he didn't hesitate to accept. For some time, he had been hard at work on plans for the Imperial Hotel in Tokyo; since he would be spending many months in Japan, completing the technical details of his plans and then overseeing the construction of the hotel, he should perhaps have refused the Barnsdall commission, but there was little on the boards for him and his staff at Taliesin (his house, office, and family citadel in the Wisconsin countryside) and money was, as usual, in short supply. Moreover, Wright was always buoyantly optimistic about how much he could accomplish within a given period of time; some of the most famous of his buildings were roughed out on paper overnight and afterwards, to Wright's real or affected astonishment, took months and years to realize. It was also true that the Barnsdall commission kept expanding as client and architect talked it over. Like so many architects, Wright was a spell-binder: he kindled his clients' imaginations and gave them the courage to build – and spend – on a far more lavish scale than they had at first intended. Miss Barnsdall, whose wealth came from Oklahoma oil, was a young woman with strong convictions, one of which was that Los Angeles lacked culture. As a step towards the improvement of the city's sorry cultural state, she wished to provide it with a theatre. To begin with, Wright and she spoke of a small theatre on an ordinary city plot, but Barnsdall, catching fire, purchased a thirty-six acre site on Hollywood Boulevard at Vermont Avenue. The property, called Olive Hill, was a choice one, covering an entire city block and offering, from the summit of its little wooded hill, a view of the Pacific.

The architectural historian Esther McCoy has described Barnsdall as Wright's most difficult client. There may be a number of ghosts throughout the country who would like to rise up and challenge that opinion, protesting vehemently, "No, no! *I* was!" Be that as it may, Barnsdall and Wright were certainly equals in pride and arbitrariness. As an heiress, Barnsdall was accustomed to changing her mind whenever she pleased; as a genius, Wright was accustomed to assuming that he knew a client's mind better than the client did. The contract for the Barnsdall project was a very substantial one, by Wright's or any other architect's standards – three hundred and seventy-five thousand dollars, architect's fees included. (A little over a decade earlier, the luxurious Gamble house had cost fifty thousand dollars.) It was too important a project for Wright to risk losing, and probably it was just as well that most of the innumerable disagreements that took place between him and Barnsdall over the succeeding three or four years were by mail and telegram and not in person. Barnsdall traveled incessantly and Wright was mostly in Japan, but each had a lieutenant on the spot – in Barnsdall's case, a business manager, and in Wright's case a young Viennese protégé named R. M. Schindler, soon to launch a brilliant architectural career of his own. Slowly there rose on Olive

22, 23. The low height of small houses in Los Angeles is far more noticeable today than it was when they were built, thanks in part to the lavish vegetation that now flourishes all round them and in part, still more bizarrely, to the skyscraping cubes of office-buildings that, at first glance, seem to leap straight up out of their modest rooftrees.

Hill the main residence, known as Hollyhock House, and several subsidiary buildings, but, by an irony, no theatre: the culture of Los Angeles had to get along as best it could without the help of the mercurial Barnsdall.

In 1923, Wright was living in Los Angeles (what he called "domestic infelicity" kept him at a distance from Taliesin), and during the course of the next year or so he designed several other houses there. They are curious structures, at once arrogant and defensive, shutting out the world around them and inventing a new world within their walls – a world that, though new, seems to echo many ancient civilizations, whether real or imaginary. Unlike the Greene brothers, who sought to marry their houses to the surrounding landscape, Wright's California houses tend to dominate the landscape, accommodating themselves not so much to terrain as to climate. Even the Millard house, tucked away in a ravine among high eucalyptus trees, fastidiously separates itself from its neighbors, while the Ennis house, resting its immense, fortress-like weight on top of a hill, startles us into a recollection of what Wright once wrote about the building of his first Taliesin: "I knew well that no house should ever be *on* a hill or *on* anything . . . Taliesin was to be an abstract combination of stone and wood as they naturally met in the aspect of

25. (Right) In Beverly Hills, Bel Air, and Brentwood, architects in the nineteen-twenties were encouraged to try their hands at a variety of styles; Tudor was one of them. In communities that had sprung up almost overnight, peopled in large measure by rootless newcomers, what could be more reassuring than to appear to possess four-hundred-year-old roots, borrowed from some secluded valley in the Cotswolds? If mock-Tudor failed to do the trick, there were plenty of other models to choose from, including such native American models as Mount Vernon, which exists in several accurate replicas throughout the area.

24. (Left) The courtyard of the house designed by Lloyd Wright, illustrated on pages 60, 61 and 62.

the hills around about. The lines of the hills were the lines of the roofs, the slopes of the hills their slopes . . ." Plainly, if only for the time being, Wright felt obliged to make an exceptionally strong personal statement through his work, as if to say, "Here I wonderfully and singularly am. Make what you can of me, you underlings!"

At this time, too, Wright was engaged in devising a system of construction with concrete blocks that he hoped would help to revolutionize the conventional methods of building houses. All his life he was to look for materials that were cheap, abundant, and easy for unskilled labor to handle, but the search proved in large measure unfruitful. What was interesting about the intricately patterned concrete blocks he designed was how little "natural" they looked; they caught the eye, and were intended to catch the eye, precisely because they did not provide, as he wrote of Taliesin, the "kind of house that would belong to that hill, as trees and rock ledges did". And because his houses were nearly always an adventure in novel construction as well as in design, the workmanship was likely to be imperfect: roofs leaked, sashes rattled in their frames, and between the bottom of a door and its threshold snakes and other small creatures were known to make their way. Once at a dinner party at Charles Greene's house, Wright exclaimed admiringly, "Charles, how in the world do you do it?", which was to say, "How in the world do you get such exquisite workmanship in your houses?" The answer was that the Greenes had trained a small army of skilled artisans to carry out their work; this small army was deployed mostly in and around Pasadena, and the cost of it was borne by wealthy clients. Wright built houses wherever he happened to be invited to,

26, 27. (Left and above) Shortly after the turn of the century, a real-estate promoter named Abbot Kinney, who had helped to develop Santa Monica, conceived the romantic notion of building a new Venice on the shores of the Pacific, modeled as closely as possible upon the old. To that end, he bought up some otherwise largely unusable wetlands, dug canals, and built (in wood) a few arcaded Italianate structures and a long pier extending out to sea, on which a sizeable theatre was erected.

Kinney dreamed of making Venice into a citadel of upper-class culture, but the upper classes went elsewhere and by the late twenties the dream had come to an end in ignoble fiscal disarray. Most of the canals subsequently silted in and the gondolas that once floated upon them rotted away at their inaccessible *imbarcaderos*. By an irony, culture – in the form of artists, writers, and sculptors – currently flourishes in Venice, which poverty has preserved as it once unwittingly preserved the original.

with local workmen hired hit-or-miss, and usually with less money in the budget than the project would turn out to require.

Of the young architects who worked under Wright in California in the twenties, one was his first-born son, Lloyd Wright. He had been trained as a landscape architect by the Olmstead brothers, the most prominent landscape architects of their day, and he and his father between them designed the landscaping of Olive Hill. Lloyd Wright was soon designing houses on his own, many of which bore a striking family resemblance to the houses of the senior Wright. For himself and his family, he built on Doheny Drive a snug little cave of a house, now owned by his son Eric. Frank Lloyd Wright is said by Eric to have admired the house, and no wonder: his stamp is in every cranny. Later, Lloyd Wright was to follow his bent in a less obviously filial fashion; an extremely popular architect, he designed scores of buildings in and around Los Angeles, two of the most celebrated of them being the Sowden house, in Hollywood (currently nicknamed "Jaws", in tribute to its shark-like open entrance-way), and the Wayfarer's Chapel, in Palos Verdes.

As a student in Vienna of the architect-teacher Adolph Loos, R. M. Schindler had early come to admire the works of Frank Lloyd Wright, and in 1914 he arrived in America with the promise of a job in an architectural firm in Chicago. After a few years there, he felt ready to journey to Taliesin and all but demand that Wright put him on the payroll. Wright at last consented to do so, but "payroll" was more often than not a metaphor; room and board, yes, by all means, but actual money was scant. When Wright went off to Tokyo, he dispatched Schindler (who by then had acquired a wife) to Los Angeles, to oversee the construction taking place on Olive Hill. With Wright's approval by mail, Schindler, who had been allowed to design little more than a chicken-coop at Taliesin, designed a couple of the subsidiary buildings at Olive Hill and then set himself up in practice. Like so many young architects, he was for a time his own best client. With the financial help of his wife's father, land was purchased on Kings Road, in West Hollywood, and Schindler set about designing a one-story house of concrete and wood, containing two separate apartments joined by a common kitchen. One apartment would be occupied by the Schindlers, the other by a friend and engineering associate who would share their interests as well as the kitchen – a risky proposition. The house was intended to be built with as little skilled labor as possible. The side-walls consisted of four-foot-wide panels of concrete. The concrete was poured into wooden forms on the ground and, when hard, lifted upright by means of a derrick; narrow panes of fixed glass filled the interstices between the panels. According to Esther McCoy, Schindler wrote to his friend Richard Neutra in Vienna, who was then working for Eric Mendelsohn, "My house is finished – that is, I live in it and work on the interior. The money ran out before everything was finished and now I have to finish it myself." Surely a hundred young architect-owners, or a thousand, have penned that last sentence over the years, in mingled pride and desperation!

The Schindlers entertained a great deal in their little house. The first tenant left, but an unending stream of new ones moved in; some paid rent and some didn't. After the Schindlers had a child, some odd little cubicles, which Schindler called "sleeping baskets", were affixed to the flat roof in order to increase the amount of living space. At Schindler's urging, in 1924 Neutra and his wife and child abandoned the Old World for the New, Neutra finding work in Chicago with the firm of Holabird & Roche. The Neutras visited with Wright at Taliesin and in 1926 dropped in without warning at the Schindlers', where they remained for several years. At first, the two architects worked companionably together, but soon they drew apart, not without reason. In architecture perhaps more than in any other profession the hazards of rivalry are hard to mitigate. This is especially true if one is practicing avant-garde architecture – a field of activity in which clients sufficiently adventurous and sufficiently rich are always difficult to find. Wright, for example, often felt betrayed by his disciples, Schindler among them. He suspected Schindler of having taken advantage of his absence in Japan to gain favor with Barnsdall and other actual or prospective clients. Now Schindler came to feel, with far more justification, that Neutra was following a similar course with him.

Schindler's best clients were Leah and Philip Lovell, for whom in 1925–26

28. Wit in the street furniture of Los Angeles consists largely of unexpected appositions. What have this mailbox, this lion, and this pillar in common except that they have happened to please the fancy of the property-owner who placed them there? The pillar is especially implausible; the lion may be thought to be guarding the mailbox, but the pillar supports nothing – appears, indeed, to find some difficulty in supporting itself.

29–32. The facades of the houses in comparatively new sections of the city – including one that bears the self-congratulatory name of Mount Olympus – do what they can to live up to their imagined lofty classical Greek past. To put it coarsely, the gods never had it so good.

he designed a house at Newport Beach that has long since entered architectural history. Subsequently, he prepared plans for a house to be built by the Lovells on a Los Angeles hilltop; the Lovells rejected these plans in favor of a design by the newcomer Neutra. Schindler and Neutra had jointly entered an international competition for the design of a new headquarters building for the League of Nations, in Geneva; they had failed to win the competition, but their plans aroused interest and in the course of time Neutra high-handedly arrogated to himself the full credit for them. The two men parted angrily, and many years later Schindler told McCoy that for Neutra the gaining of the commission for the Lovell house was a forgivable act of self-survival, "but the removal of [Schindler's] name from their League of Nations entry was an act of malice." They remained estranged until, in 1953, they were placed by chance in the same room at the Cedars of Lebanon Hospital; Neutra was recovering from a heart-attack and Schindler from a second operation on the cancer that was soon to kill him. In the hospital, McCoy tells us, they had long talks "and laughed about Vienna and their contemporaries." What a pleasing glimpse of Schindler we are offered here! For to be able to laugh and revive an old friendship in the imminent presence of death is no small feat, and it is one that Neutra was almost certainly incapable of. In his case, as death approached he busied himself with falsifying the facts of his career, bringing them ever closer to his heart's desire.

It has to be said for this fiercely ambitious man that however he managed to secure the commission for the Lovell house (in the beginning, the Lovells were under the impression that Schindler and Neutra were designing the house together), he produced a masterpiece – the earliest and still one of the most vivid examples of what has come to be known as "high-tech" architecture. At work in Chicago, Neutra had been fascinated to discover how much that went into the making of a building in America could be ordered from Sweet's catalogue, and the Lovell house is exquisite not in spite of the industrial components out of which it was largely created but because of them. It floats in space over its little valley like some delicate craft from outer space that has made a safe land-fall and is content to remain tethered by a steel and concrete bridge to a nearby road. The interior contains several prankish salutes to industrial mass production, including a sink from a Pullman sleeping-car and a Model A Ford headlight, countersunk into the wall of the main staircase.

Oddly enough, the Lovells, who found that the beach house by Schindler suited them to perfection, were ill content with the far grander city house by Neutra. Its fame gave them a measure of fame as well, and yet in 1958 Mrs Lovell told McCoy, "I never felt that I belonged to the house," and Lovell added, "It had no lilt, no happiness, no joy." Contemporary visitors to the house are apt to like it better than the Lovells remembered liking it, and one wonders whether the gloomy view they took of it in age may not have been based in part on the fact that they moved into the house in October, 1929, just as the stock-market crash on Wall Street was ushering in the Great Depression that would last for many years and would put an end to the Lovells' building adventures. They had had to borrow a great deal of money to finance the unexpectedly high cost of the house – the Lovells had assumed that Neutra was

33–35. In Los Angeles, a severely correct imitation of an eighteenth-century French chateau is likely to arouse more astonishment among architectural historians than a pure fantasy like the so-called "witch's house", which was built in 1921 by Irvin V. Willat. An early movie cameraman, director, and producer, Willat was known for his pioneering experiments with special effects. The house was designed by Willat's art director, Harry C. Oliver, to serve as a movie studio, an administration building, and a sort of three-dimensional "logo" for Willat's vaulting imagination. It was erected in Culver City originally but later moved to Beverly Hills. Its calculatedly tumble-down appearance caused a sensation when it was built, as an embodiment of the Hollywood hope that any fantasy, however extreme, was likely to prosper.

Between the extremes of "La Bagatelle" and cloud-cuckooland, a modestly conventional bungalow assumes a certain dignity.

a shrewder calculator of budgets than Schindler was, and this proved not to be the case – and the house became for them, in Lovell's words, "an albatross".

After half a century and despite a number of unlucky alterations, the house asserts itself with undiminished self-confidence upon its characteristically implausible Los Angeles site: a hillside so steep that the vertical framing of the house, which has three stories, is equivalent to that of an eight- or nine-story building. The intricacy of the plan is hinted at in the boldly asymmetrical elevations; various areas of the house and grounds – living quarters, working quarters, sleeping quarters, servants' quarters, garden, and swimming pool – are as neatly fitted together as the works of some gigantic watch; one listens for a telltale tick. The living quarters are full of sunlight and air. Neutra's manipulations of space are both practical and lyrical; big as the Lovell house is, it could be contentedly lived in by a single individual.

A quarter of a century later, in Pasadena, Neutra designed a house for Constance Perkins that, though perhaps a tenth the size of the Lovell house, was equally practical, equally lyrical. Lovell had complained of Neutra's damnable "Germanic" precision – everything had to be laid out just so and was intended to remain just so forever – but Miss Perkins (for many years and to this day a member of the faculty of Occidental College) welcomed this precision, understanding that the smaller the house the more deftly everything must dovetail. The commission might seem a small one, but Neutra took infinite pains in ascertaining Miss Perkins' housekeeping requirements and then in ascertaining the degree to which they matched his aesthetic requirements. Did she, for example, wash her dishes after breakfast or leave them stacked up in the sink, perhaps to be joined by dishes from lunch and dinner? If she washed them immediately, then Neutra would permit the kitchen window to be placed next to the front door; if she left them stacked, then he would make sure that people at the front door would have no kitchen window nearby, since in his opinion the sight of her slovenly culinary arrangements might well prove sickening to them. Luckily for Miss Perkins, she was accustomed to washing her dishes after every meal; her sink is within easy view of the front door, and a spotless sink it is. The Perkins house is no less a masterpiece than the Lovell house, and it is only fair to say of Neutra that he wasn't altogether tyrannical in the designing of it: the shape of the little ornamental pool that passes unobtrusively through a sheet of glass from outside the house to inside was sketched by an art student in one of Miss Perkins' classes.

Neutra was to have many more followers than Schindler and to make a far louder noise in the world, but even Neutra was often hard-pressed to find suitable clients. For both new money and old money have a natural tendency to favor convention over novelty, old money because it knows no better than not to take chances and new money because it hopes that by not taking chances it will be mistaken for old. In Southern California before the First World War, novelty in architecture was embodied not only in the work of the Greene brothers but also in that of Irving J. Gill, who took the reigning Mission style and the Spanish Colonial style that was then coming into fashion and twisted them so dextrously out of shape that few of his clients appear to

36–39. (Right) Joinery designed by the Greene brothers. A deliberate archaism and superb finish characterize every detail of their work. (Overleaf) A house they designed in 1908, at the height of their success, for the Gamble family of Cincinnati. It is located at 4 Westmoreland Place, in Pasadena, which in the early years of this century was a favorite winter resort of wealthy families from the Middle West, bent upon escaping the bitter cold and heavy snows of that region. The Gambles were admirable clients, not only because they were rich but also because they gave the Greenes a free hand in the actual building of the house. Off they went to Japan on an extended trip and the house was more or less ready for them to move into on their return. (The Greenes themselves never visited Japan.) Given by descendants of the Gambles to the University of Southern California and open to the public, the house is an ideal example of the quality of workmanship that the Greenes were able to secure from a crew of artisans whom they had trained and whom they kept constantly in their employ. The house sits on a slight rise, with a terrace at the rear overlooking a valley. A grassy berm was built in front of the house in order to conceal from the casual passerby on Westmoreland Place most of the brick driveway that leads to the front door. Much of the furniture in the house – including an upright piano in the living-room, just to the right of the entrance – was designed by the Greenes.

have been aware of how daring they were in consenting to live in such highly original houses.

As David Gebhard and Robert Winter point out in their exhaustive, delightful "Guide to the Architecture of Los Angeles and Southern California", Gill took care to make his clients feel that they were remaining respectably within bounds by providing them with pergolas, tiled porches, and white masonry walls, set in a bower of vines and flowering shrubs. Gill also painted the wooden trim around his windows and doors with a peculiar blue-green paint that struck a decorous note of tropical sensuality. But his decorum deceives, as does the seeming modesty of his intentions. Henry James said once that a building that sits is more pleasing than a building that stands; Gill's houses sit, and with not a whit less assurance than those of his more flamboyant contemporaries. There is an odd, quiet power about them, and they give the impression that they would rather explode than give away the secret of that power.

After the First World War, novelty in architecture was to be looked for in the work of Frank Lloyd Wright, Lloyd Wright, Schindler, Neutra, and their unruly and diverse followers, while convention was to be looked for in the imperturbably tasteful pastiches of such able architects as Wallace Neff, Paul R. Williams, and Reginald Johnson. Again and again, what handsome buildings they brought into the world! Those were the days, in the twenties and thirties, when clients fancied a wide range of historic backdrops against which to act out the calm or stormy melodramas of their lives: Tudor, Stuart, Georgian, Regency, Norman, Italian Baroque, perhaps a hint here of Swiss chalet, or a hint there of Cotswold farmhouse. An architect who had grown up in the Beaux-Arts tradition felt no loss of personal integrity in being required to make his up-to-the-minute plans assume in elevation one or another of a score of nostalgic Old World disguises. He would be sure to have his preference among styles and he would press this style upon clients, but in the end it was the client who held the purse-strings and who had his way.

Los Angeles is celebrated not only for its high proportion of private dwellings but also for the fact that these dwellings change hands so often over the years. In Boston and Philadelphia – even in New York City – it is a commonplace for families to occupy the same house for seventy or eighty years; in Los Angeles, a decade is a long time. There are several reasons for this, perhaps first among them the rueful truth that many elderly people come to Southern California, hoping to make a long-held dream come true; they arrive at a moment when death is just about to interrupt the dream, and the trim little house in Lemon Grove proves to be but a temporary resting place between Iowa and Forest Lawn. Another reason is that the ancient economic principle of easy come, easy go operates with exceptionally high efficiency in Los Angeles. Movie stars in the twenties grew rich overnight, as rock stars do today; they also grew poor overnight. Harold Lloyd, who is reputed to have earned some thirty thousand dollars a week in the twenties, built himself a Mediterranean villa, which he continued to occupy until his death, growing daily richer and richer from his investments in Los Angeles real estate. But

40, 41. (Above and right) The owners of Greene & Greene houses, like the owners of houses designed by Stanford White or Frank Lloyd Wright, are expected to feel a certain sense of camaraderie. They have come into possession of something not entirely their own – something they must be willing to share with each other and with the world at large. The Blacker house (detail, right) was built several years after the Gamble house (above), and the architectural historians Gebhard and Winter argue that it is less fine, but the houses have much in common, not least the fact that both of them are much less adventurous in plan than they are in elevation.

42–44. (Overleaf) On the left, the terrace of the Gamble house. Tile, brick, uncut rocks, wood, bronze, and copper – all the ingredients that might have been met with in an Oriental temple two or three thousand years ago contentedly mingle with one another and with the soft green landscape of contemporary Pasadena. (Right) Many of the same timeless elements are present in the luxurious ranch-house designed and occupied by the architect Cliff May. In the Mays' vast living-room, the meeting of indoors and outdoors is more ancient Roman than ancient Oriental; a wealthy senator in the time of Caesar Augustus might have owned a villa much like this in the Sabine hills, with an atrium open to the sky and a fountain splashing its welcome by the front door.

Lloyd was an exception: his friend Buster Keaton went from rags to riches and back to rags in a period of a few years and died destitute, as did Fatty Arbuckle and a dozen other early movie stars.

Architects in Southern California have long been accustomed to designing a house for a client and then redesigning it not once but several times, for a succession of clients. A house that appears to have been built in 1980 may be found to be, under closer examination, a sort of palimpsest, containing evidence here and there – a heavily moulded Elizabethan plaster ceiling, say,

in what was once a library and is now a rumpus room – of earlier incarnations. Remodelings are easier to carry out on the conventional houses of the twenties and thirties than they would be on the severe and elegant houses (children and grandchildren of the International Style) that were put up in the period after the Second World War. An immaculate house of steel and glass by Craig Ellwood or Pierre Koenig is tampered with at one's peril; even a hot-tub in an adjacent garden may throw the entire composition into disarray. In their shining suavity, they would rather be consumed by some midsummer blaze leaping from canyon to canyon and reducing their walls to mere squiggles of molten cullet than to have added to them the now obligatory TV room and indoor barbeque pit, complete with gabled roof and Grecian doorway.

Ellwood and Koenig, along with Raphael S. Soriano, Gregory Ain, J. R. Davidson, and a number of other architects, were participants in what was surely the most important experiment in domestic architecture to be carried out in Southern California after the Second World War – the so-called Case Study House program, which ran from 1945 to 1960 and was the brain-child of John Entenza, editor of a magazine called "California Arts and Architecture". According to Gebhard and Winter, although none

45, 46. Tucked away on a steep hillside leading off Santa Monica Canyon are log cabins built half a century ago by members of the Uplifters Club – a group of businessmen from downtown Los Angeles, whose idea of uplift was very unlike that of the many Methodist ministers then living in that neighborhood. Uplift to the Uplifters meant raising a glass of gin or whiskey in the privacy of their snug little weekend hideaways, in defiance of the deplorable state of affairs known as Prohibition. The cabins have an odd air of being diminished versions of the great camps of the Adirondacks. Wood that has been crudely fashioned or, where possible, left in a natural state, serves to provide benches, cases for clocks, and handrails for stairs. Arriving in Cadillacs and Packards, the Uplifters played at being pioneers.

54

47, 48. (Above and right) Frank Lloyd Wright came to Los Angeles in the early nineteen-twenties, hoping to establish a substantial practice there. The adventure proved to be something of a misadventure, but a few houses from his hand – among the most curious that he ever designed – survive to be admired and speculated about. His biggest commission came from Aline Barnsdall, an oil millionairess, who wished a veritable village of assorted buildings to crown her property, Olive Hill.

She and Wright quarreled incessantly, but with fruitful consequences: her residence, Hollyhock House, is a monument to both of them. Wright had prepared the plans for Hollyhock House while still at work on the Imperial Hotel, in Japan. The house was built under the supervision of R. M. Schindler, who also designed a building on the property (with Wright's approval) and later, with Richard J. Neutra, a wading pool and pergola.

49. From the beginning, Miss Barnsdall had intended that Olive Hill should serve some substantial cultural purpose in the life of Los Angeles; the air evoked by Hollyhock House and its attendant buildings was never meant to reflect a cozy domestic felicity. The relationship of interior and exterior spaces is ceremonial. In the company of a sufficient number of people, one feels awe, but alone one might well feel intimidated. Eventually, Miss Barnsdall gave Olive Hill to the city; it now functions as the Municipal Art Gallery.

50. (Right) Coming to America from Vienna in the twenties, Richard J. Neutra was filled with admiration for the industrial components that one could order out of a catalogue and put to highly practical – and handsome – use in private dwellings. In the thirties, he designed the Lovell house in Los Angeles; to the greatest possible extent, the materials out of which it is so artfully composed are stock items. Even the round electric light countersunk into the wall of the stair came off a warehouse shelf – it is a Model A Ford headlight.

of the architects involved in the program pandered to what was assumed to be the popular taste of the time, the first six houses to be opened to the public drew an attendance of something over three hundred and fifty thousand people and the completed program had a profound effect upon the architecture of the entire state and, indirectly, upon that of the country at large. The Case Study houses were intended to be works of art as well as habitations and they prompted a similarly lofty intention in respect to their furnishings – for example, chairs by Charles Eames and Marcel Breuer passed from being the favorite possessions of a small elite to being readily recognizable objects in the marketplace, often imitated and, alas, coarsened by inexpensive manufacture.

By the nineteen-sixties, most of the bold gestures of innovation and accommodation had been carried out – not new themes but variations on accepted themes became the order of the day. If in the thirties and forties architects as gifted as Harwell Hamilton Harris had learned to soften and somewhat sentimentalize Wright by imposing a measure of decorum upon his excesses, in the sixties and seventies John Lautner has been sentimentalizing Wright by emphasizing his excesses. Not so much Wright's virtues as Wright's faults are brought to mind by, say, Lautner's cliff-hanging "Silvertop" house, which looks out over Silver Lake and threatens to pitch headlong into it, or even his so-called Chemosphere House, floating on its single high steel stalk like some gigantic glassy dandelion in full bloom, carried in from outer space by who knows what unlooked-for breeze. There are eccentricities galore in contemporary Los Angeles, but few surprises. The up-to-the-minute elegance of Peter de Bretteville's "high-tech" house offers not the shock of novelty but the shock of recognition: we think at once of Neutra's Lovell house, and of the Eames house in its grassy meadow above the Pacific.

An innovation sufficiently prolonged becomes a fashion and a fashion sufficiently prolonged becomes a style. California has long prided itself on initiating fashions, whether in swimsuits, tax-cuts, or religious sects, and it is certainly the case that at least twice in this century a distinctively Californian style of architecture has spread from coast to coast: the California bungalow style, which flourished before and just after the First World War and was characterized by low, broad gables and porch roofs supported on stubby columns of brick or wood; and the California ranch-house style, which has been gaining in popularity continuously since the end of the Second World War. (Specimens of a third style, a California version of Spanish Colonial, can often be found in large cities, in real-estate developments laid out prior to 1929 and the subsequent depression; they are rare in cities with populations of fewer than twenty-five thousand people and in certain areas, such as New England, they are almost non-existent.) As one approaches the East coast, where open land is hard to come by and therefore expensive and where the rigor of winter requires substantial central heating, the California ranch-house tends to draw in upon itself, making up in height what it lacks in breadth. From this huddled posture springs the curious neologism, "splanch", which one encounters daily in the real-estate sections of Eastern newspapers and which stands for "split-level ranch". "Splanch" usually means that a couple of

51. Topiary mailboxes on Muirfield Road.

bedrooms and a bathroom have been fitted into a second story above a partly subterranean garage; it may also mean that a "family" room has been added to the usual living room, though the difference between what goes on in a family room and in a living room remains undefined – one suspects that the living room becomes the formal preserve of visitors. There are ranch-houses and splanch-houses all the way out to the furthermost rocky tip of Long Island, cleaving the Atlantic, and they seem not uncomfortable there (especially as the sun and the sea air gradually weather them), but one is tempted to assert that their natural setting is the Pacific coast; it is a Pacific climate and a Pacific culture that have brought them into being.

That dictum uttered, a formidable exception immediately springs to mind. By far the most skillful practitioner of the California ranch-house style is Cliff

52–54. Frank Lloyd Wright found his stay in Southern California less fruitful than he had hoped, but his sons John and Lloyd both settled in Los Angeles in the early nineteen-twenties and prospered there. Like his father before him, John Wright was precocious: he was executing commissions of some importance at the age of nineteen. Lloyd Wright, the first-born son, began his career as a landscape architect in the distinguished firm of Olmsted & Olmsted and then made his way gradually into domestic architecture. This house, which Lloyd Wright designed in 1926, obviously owes a good deal to the senior Wright's experiments with pre-cast concrete block, carried out a short time before. After more than fifty years of exposure to sun, wind, and rain, the blocks have the look of being all that remains of some ancient, long-lost Central American civilization – no doubt the very effect that Wright was seeking. The front entrance is beneath a formidable arrangement of concrete and glass, which Derry Moore was quick to nickname "Jaws". And it is true that one feels as if one were entering some vast behemoth as one passes into a dark vestibule and up a gullet-like flight of steps to the main floor.

55. The interior of the house illustrated on pages 60 and 61.

May, who in the course of a career that began in 1932 has designed ranch-houses in uncounted hundreds of different localities, most of them in California but some of them as far afield as Australia, Venezuela, Switzerland, Ireland, Italy, and several islands in the Caribbean. Ranch-houses by May, modified to accommodate to climate and topography, are to be found in forty-five of our fifty states; during a brief period in the early nineteen-fifties, he licensed on a fee basis to builders plans for a low-cost ranch-house, of which no fewer than eighteen thousand were built and sold. Of his individually designed ranch-houses, May estimates that they run into well over a thousand. Given the total number of May houses designed and built to date, it could be argued that May is probably the most popular architect who has ever lived. In books of architectural history, the tiny Eames house will no doubt take pride of place over the grandest of May's ranch-houses, but no matter. The quantity of work he has presided over is hard to take in; the quality of much of it is, under the circumstances, astonishingly high.

A true ranch-house of the nineteenth century was the main structure in a cluster of buildings that were flung up any which way over a period of years. May has perfected an apparent randomness of plan that convincingly resembles that cluster and evokes the simplicities of an earlier, more hospitable, and (we may pretend) more affectionate time. Rooms flow into one another and out onto terraces and enclosed patios; it is always an agreeable sensation to lose one's way not once but several times in getting from the front door of a May house to a distant bedroom. The bigger the ranch-house, the greater the opportunity: May's own house, at the head of a long canyon within the city limits but seeming to lie in some remote valley of the High Sierra (one hears from a nearby pasture the whinnying of horses, the baying of hounds), might be mistaken at first glance for a village. The scale is big but unintimidating. The living-room, for example, is fifty-five feet long, thirty-five feet wide, and fifteen feet high at the skylighted crest of its "cathedral" ceiling. It contains two grand pianos, thousands of ancient vellum-bound books, folk sculpture from half a dozen cultures, and innumerable oversized couches, tables, and chairs. Hard as it may be to believe, the room is cozily domestic, inviting one to rough it ranch-house style on a very high level of luxury. If one sits in the patio under the stars and the night air grows cold, underfoot the paving is warm; whether indoors or out, May takes care to provide heat when nature doesn't. Away in the dark, one hears the hissing of water in the thick ground-cover of a distant hillside. That, too, is May's handiwork; a miniature rain-forest flourishes where for months no rain is likely to fall. Closer to hand, the splash of a fountain, the glint of firelight on a grilled Spanish casement. Sparks fly up out of a crumbling pyramid of logs; the logs are real and so is the concealed jet of gas that keeps them flaring.

At the foot of the canyon road stretches a city of many millions, ablaze with lights, throbbing with activity. The quiet house and its accompaniment of shadowy fields and woods is a stage-set, but the wise student of Los Angeles perceives – and is content to perceive – that a stage-set is no more true or false than the dream it embodies. All those hundreds upon hundreds of May ranch-houses, big and small, like all the hundreds of thousands of anonymous dwellings that make up the loosely woven fabric of the city, are embodiments of dreams that, against high odds, have managed to come true. Wracked by floods, droughts, and earthquakes, in terms of safety Los Angeles might just as well be perched on the simmering upper slopes of Vesuvius, but it doesn't matter: nothing is as outrageous and everlasting as a dream, and a city founded on dreams and scorning prudence is likely to endure forever.

56. Frank Lloyd Wright designed the Ennis house in 1924, on the brow of a hill so steep that from the valley below the structure appears to be a gigantic Mayan ziggurat, not to be approached except perhaps by parachute. At close range, one sees that the house is capable of being penetrated in a conventional fashion. The front entrance, which faces an ample motor court, is, as usual with Wright, very low; he was a short man and tall men often had to duck in making their way through a Wright building. To the left is a glimpse of a scrub-covered hillside characteristic of Los Angeles. Wright's formidable pile of masonry – concrete blocks knit together by steel links – was intended to dominate this often pitilessly sunny landscape and establish a refuge from it by means of large, dim spaces concealed within fortress-like walls (see following 7 plates).

57–60. (Left, above and overleaf) A question well worth pondering: what did the owners of Wright's more exotic domestic structures make of them? Because Wright could charm birds out of trees, many a client found himself with a house totally unlike the one he intended to build. Nevertheless, it appears to be the case that from very early in Wright's career a client's pride in possessing a house by Wright nearly always outweighed the practical difficulties that such a house was likely to impose. Leaky roofs were a commonplace of Wright's designs; so (especially in his late years) were tiny kitchens. As for furnishing a Wright house, the Master rejoiced to assume the task whenever he was permitted to, often enough with deplorable results. Many of the chairs he designed are not only miserably uncomfortable but have a tendency to pitch the sitter backwards, head over heels onto a hard floor. His houses look their best when they contain as little furniture as possible.

61–63. Though Wright preached the goodness of a simple agrarian culture, he felt a characteristic nineteenth-century relish for technological progress. He was always quick to exploit the latest developments in electric lighting, plumbing, heating, the efficient sheltering of automobiles, and the use of swimming pools as part of the overall design of a house. (The high wall of the Ennis pool helps to screen it from the adjacent road.) Subtle methods of indirect lighting were a particular interest of Wright's at least from the Robie house on. In the Ennis house, light emerges from within the pierced concrete blocks and toggle-plates are given a dignified place in the design.

64, 65. Eccentrics, so common abroad, are a rarity in America. One of our most notable was Howard Hughes, who in age became a recluse, shuffling about with his bare feet stuck into empty Kleenex boxes in order to avoid contamination by germs. In his youth, he was a zealous playboy as well as a brilliant businessman, but he early reached an age at which he feared being bored by women and places; he needed an ample number of both to keep him at attention. In Los Angeles, he is said to have maintained a variety of hideaways, one of which is pictured here (left). From the street, only a nondescript carport is visible; behind it a sizeable house has been built into the side of a cliff. Vegetation springs naturally out of the earth, sheltered from adverse weather by an unobtrusive skylight. The pin-up painting may have begun existence in a local nightclub and is probably post-Hughes; Hughes' taste was not high, but it was higher than this oil.

66, 67. (Right and overleaf) In 1931, a wealthy dentist named Atwater commissioned the architect Robert Stacy-Judd to design a small colony of inexpensive houses in the "Pueblo Revival" style. The effect was charming, but the idea didn't catch on, perhaps because the Depression was then at its grimmest and few people were seeking novelty even at low cost.

The thick walls and comparatively small windows of the pueblo style are appropriate to the semi-arid climate of Los Angeles; they help to ward off the fierceness of the sun, but since most Angelinos are sun-worshippers this seeming advantage has always gone for naught. Many artists, sculptors, and ceramicists have enjoyed living in the Atwater colony, in part because of its air of rural remoteness; suavely glittering Wilshire Boulevard might be a thousand miles away.

68. (Right) The Atwater houses, dun-colored like elephants, rise at the edge of Elysian Park, which boasts an aboriginal density of forest and undergrowth. In early movie days, the Park often "stood in" for Africa and other not very plausible locations. Children growing up in this apparent wilderness in the very heart of Los Angeles follow a way of life not altogether different from that of Mark Twain on the banks of the Mississippi long ago. Tom Sawyer and his friend Huck might have built this tree-house and, spending the night in it, scared themselves half to death with ghost stories.

69–71. Virginia and Gerald Oppenheimer live in a house built by Tom Mix, a famous cowboy movie star of the twenties. Mix was second only to Douglas Fairbanks in the daring acrobatic feats that he performed, mostly on horseback, for the purpose of rescuing honorable men from scoundrels and maidens from dire fates. When it came to choosing an architectural style worthy of his improved station in life, Mix turned to Tudor, perhaps on the assumption that what was good enough for Henry VIII might well prove good enough for him. The Oppenheimers have de-Tudorized the house and transformed its gardens, which now march wittily down a steep slope by means of a series of bleacher-like platforms, profusely planted. In turning a mock-Tudor mansion into a contemporary house, the Oppenheimers have cleverly preserved a portion of the original drawing-room ceiling, with its ornate plasterwork. Mix is said on occasion to have ridden his horse straight into the drawing-room – again, a gesture worthy of a Tudor.

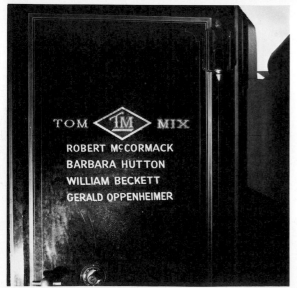

72. (Above) In his business pursuits, Mr Oppenheimer makes use of a computer that he has programmed to converse with him in highly colloquial terms; if he asks it an unsatisfactory question, the computer invites him to "knock it off" or relax and have a cup of coffee.

73. (Left) The enormous weight of safes is such that they are rarely moved; the biography of this safe is told by the succession of names lettered upon its surface.

74. (Right) Chairs on the Oppenheimer terrace cluster together as if for companionship while the human members of the household are elsewhere.

75–77. The Lovell house seems to float up out of its little secret valley with a minimum of support, the upper stories overhanging the lower ones. In designing it, Richard Neutra evidently wished us to imagine the house as placing the least possible weight upon the land it occupies; one thinks of Frank Lloyd Wright's "Falling Water", in Pennsylvania, and of how it, too, hangs in delicate balance *above* its site and not upon it. Over the years, some of the open balconies of the Lovell house have been glassed in; it must have looked even more ethereal in the thirties than it does today. In contrast to the elevations, the plan of the house is rigorously down-to-earth: a place for everything and everything in its place. The house appears to have proved insufficiently impromptu for the Lovells, who moved elsewhere.

When Neutra first came to America, he fell upon a copy of Sweet's Catalogue with something like the ardor of a fundamentalist Christian falling upon a copy of the Old Testament. Here were thousands of items of manufacture waiting to be ordered and put to immediate use; an entire house could be fashioned out of a book! The small dentist's hand-basin in an upper hall of the Lovell house was ordered from a catalog. It is not of a practical size, but it is charming. In principle, what is mass-produced and readily available ought to prove cheaper than what is hand-made and subject to the mood of the individual maker; nevertheless, the principle has almost always failed. Our houses continue to be largely hand-made and very costly.

78–80. Lloyd Wright designed this house in 1928, for his own use; it belongs today to his son Eric. Frank Lloyd Wright used to enjoy visiting the house, and no wonder: at every cranky, charming turn, it amounts to an act of filial homage. Lloyd Wright's inspiration was surely his father's experiments with pre-Columbian forms and surface designs during his California period, in the early twenties; with age, the pre-Columbian motifs have assumed a look of time-worn authenticity that they must have lacked when the mortar was still damp in the walls. The house is tiny, but the scale has been so cunningly maintained that, seated in the living-room, one looks out upon a courtyard that appears to be of considerable size and is, in fact, not much bigger than an ordinary bedroom. The Joshua tree in a corner of the courtyard appears to be immemorially old; it was planted by Lloyd Wright as a sapling, and Eric Wright suspects that its extraordinary growth may be a result of its roots having penetrated a nearby sewer line.

81–83. As we have just seen in the case of Lloyd Wright, architects are irresistibly tempted to design houses for their own use, and Thornton M. Abell has been no exception. He built this house for his family and himself in 1937 and has been living in it ever since. (To the left, Mr Abell contemplating a plant that appears to be getting out of hand.) It is a characteristic Abell arrangement to let a garage almost at curbside serve as a buffer between street and house; one steps down from the driveway to an unadorned entrance, from which the house continuously descends to a series of terraced hillside gardens. The plan is as intricate as a pocket-watch, with a number of differing floor-levels ingeniously dovetailed together. The severity of the International style, which this house and other Abell houses may be said to embody, is mitigated by ample foliage and, more subtly, by the temperament of the architect. Abell's houses have a gentleness to them in spite of their sharp edges; they are without bravado and their modesty has a lilt that makes one happy to enter them.

84. (Left) In 1955, on a rocky outcrop in Pasadena, Richard J. Neutra designed this little house for Constance Perkins, a teacher of art. (A view of the exterior of the house serves as the frontispiece of this book. The shape of the garden pool that insouciantly passes in and out of the house was created by a student of Miss Perkins, sketching at random a sequence of free forms.) The smaller the house, the more pains Neutra would take with the problem of how it was to be successfully lived in on a daily basis. He subjected Miss Perkins to a stern interrogation in regard to her housekeeping; luckily, Miss Perkins passed every test with flying colors, and, after a quarter of a century, her delightful bandbox of a house is as fresh to the eye as ever and intensely hers.

85. While Neutra was fashioning eyries out of a minimum of inexpensive materials, the Spanish Colonial Revival style continued to be admired; it was reassuringly heavy and yet romantic – a past that Americans had never known helped them to shoulder the burden of the present.

86, 87. The architect Thomas Hastings said once, "Style is the problem solved." Marion and Francis Lederer set themselves the problem of bringing into existence a house that would seem perfectly at ease with its landscape and climate, as well as with them; the style that resulted is filled with echoes of New Spain and Old, but bears no taint of a mere replica. The house and its ancillary buildings are robust and authoritative, and one would swear that they had sprung up out of the ground a long time ago, and just here, not elsewhere.

88. (Left) The kitchen of the Pasadena house pictured below has recently been redecorated, with the evident intention of employing as many disparate materials as possible, among them glass, tile, brick, Formica, and wood. The structural implausibility of a ceiling paved with brick is unnerving to anyone standing under it for the first time – what on earth is keeping gravity at bay?

89. In Pasadena, a level lawn may lead from the street to a house whose garden-side threatens to pitch headlong down the banks of a precipitous arroyo. By means of skillful landscaping, a visitor is encouraged to drift up and down a complex system of steps, terraces, and winding woodland walks, strewn with pine-needles; one might be celebrating *ferrogosto* at some villa high in the Alban hills.

90–92. A grand mansion on Sunset Boulevard, designed in the twenties by an architect imported from Paris by a wealthy French family to simulate in the still-untutored precincts of Hollywood the graces of a vanished *belle époque*. The mansion is impeccably maintained, even to a wine-cellar that few houses in contemporary Paris could hope to equal. The conservatory might be the setting for some romantic comedy by Anouilh; in the garden by the still pool whisper the ghosts of innumerable Gigis, no less to be admired for speaking "Amurrican" instead of French.

93, 94. (Overleaf) Inside the house pictured in Plates 90–92, the painted ceiling of the drawing-room hints at a vague connection with the Pavilion of the Prince Regent in Brighton. The owners have wisely elected not to conceal the graceful windows of the drawing-room behind draperies; shrubbery provides an ample amount of privacy for the house. On entering such a room, one feels an immediate impulse to push back the chairs and the tasseled rug and begin to dance – perhaps a waltz or two to start with and then a few increasingly antic polkas?

The walls and ceiling of the dining-room have been painted a glowing black. Four gilded karyatids never tire of holding upon their heads a sideboard heavy with silver and crystal, and reassuringly there leap to mind the words of Marcus Aurelius: "Even in a palace, life can be lived well."

95. (Left) One of the leading hostesses of Los Angeles is Patte Barham, author, war correspondent, and editor. She lives in a house on Fremont Place formerly occupied by James Francis Cardinal McIntyre, Archbishop of the Los Angeles diocese of the Roman Catholic Church. The house was built by King C. Gillette, in 1916, and is said with little reason to be copied in part after a royal palace in the Hawaiian Islands. In the late nineteenth century, Gillette invented the safety-razor and for several generations thereafter caused beardedness in American men to be thought eccentric.

96. (Right) Miss Barham was a close friend of Marion Davies and often visited Miss Davies and William Randolph Hearst at San Simeon. In the Barham sunroom are photographs of many of the celebrities whom Miss Barham has known.

97. (Bottom right) All carving of a certain age and of uncertain pedigree is attributed to Grinling Gibbons and this cupboard in one of the grander houses of Los Angeles has not escaped that fate. On the bottom shelf, the lion-emblem of the Swiss Guard, who die but never surrender.

98. (Left) The Taggart house, designed by Lloyd Wright between 1922 and 1924 and long occupied by the renowned movie star, Ramon Navarro. The house plunges self-confidently up the side of an almost vertical cliff and enjoys the luxury of a level prospect at its highest point. A greenish trim, stamped out of copper, provides the only decoration on the severe façade.

99. The swimming pool of the Taggart house. Lloyd Wright appears to have been able to satisfy his clients' wishes more genially than his father did; he had a large practice in the Los Angeles area and provided solutions to problems of design – including the problem of remodeling houses designed by him many years earlier – that his father would have been likely to scorn. Was this pool originally in the open air and enclosed by Wright at the behest of some later owner of the property?

100. (Above) In a niche in the Taggart house stands a bust of F. Scott Fitzgerald, hauntingly alone and out of place in a house he presumably never knew. Fitzgerald died in Los Angeles in 1940, while at work on a novel about the movie industry which he called "The Last Tycoon". Fitzgerald, Nathanael West, and Evelyn Waugh are among the few writers to give Hollywood its due.

101. (Right) A decorative lockset in the Taggart house.

102. (Opposite) The present owner of the Taggart house, in a mask of her choosing.

103, 104. One of the most exquisite of the many houses designed in Los Angeles by R. M. Schindler is the Buck house, built in 1934. Like most houses put up during the great Depression, it was small and closely reasoned in plan, with every square foot of space being put to use. A successful small house amounts to a series of optical illusions, by means of which the eye is never allowed to come to rest too soon; traversing space on a diagonal and taking unconscious note of a constant change in ceiling heights, the eye consents to perceive more space than actually exists. In the Villa Malcontenta, Palladio performed this feat on a colossal scale; Schindler performed it again and again on a tiny one.

105. (Opposite) Schindler's own house, though built long before the Depression (1921), was based on a need to practice drastic economies. It is a double house on a single level, some sleeping cabins having been fitted onto the roof at a later time. Half the house was intended to be lived in by the Schindlers, the other half by a couple who were friends of theirs. The friends soon left and the Schindlers and their one child occupied the entire premises. Neutra and Schindler had been trained in Vienna; when Neutra made his way to this country, he and his wife stayed here with the Schindlers, but the arrangement proved an unlucky one. Schindler and Neutra were both admirers of Frank Lloyd Wright and briefly his disciples; for a time, Schindler and Neutra worked as partners and then separated on unfriendly terms. They were equally gifted and between them created some of the most distinguished architecture of their time – "American" in spite of being intensely European in origin. They were of the International style, but by no means its slaves.

106. (Left) It was in Schindler's character never to grow rich and famous, never to feel that wealth and fame were necessary attributes of self-fulfillment. This little house was his Versailles and the parties he gave in it will be remembered until the last attendant at them is dead. The Schindlers were charmers, but after a while they didn't charm each other; for many years, they lived in separate quarters within the house, communicating only by an exchange of scribbled notes. And then, after long years, proof of a bond stronger than any incompatibility: during Schindler's final illness, his wife sent him an anonymous letter, praising him at his worth. And with pride Schindler read the letter aloud to friends as he lay dying.

107–109. Where the climate permits it, the apparent size of a house can be much increased by a clever marriage between exterior and interior, as we see here with the terrace of the Buck house. Many Roman villas of the first century AD appeared to be hundreds of feet long, but they consisted largely of terraces, pergolas, walled gardens, and latticed allées; the actual dwelling place might be only a series of small, darkish masonry cubes. Like Wright before him, Schindler was a Roman in the mastery with which he wove indoors and outdoors into a seamless fabric.

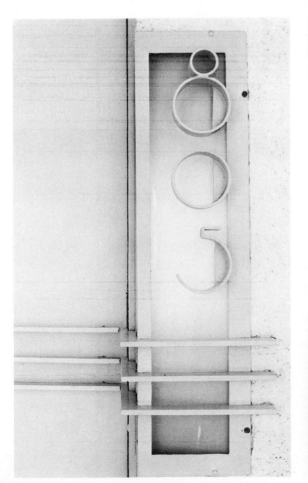

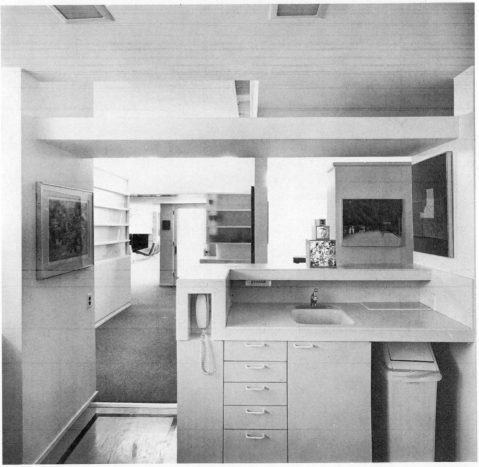

110. (Left) The sumptuous bed of the celebrated hair-stylist Vidal Sassoon. As the anthropologist Lord Raglan long ago pointed out, beds are rarely to be found throughout the world and came into existence here and there not in order to insure comfort in sleeping, as one might suppose, but for ceremonial purposes. They are outward and visible signs of the right to rule, which is why kings used to hold levées in them; they are also, in our democratic present, emblems of having arrived.

111. (Above) The Sassoon gymnasium. One of the few symbols of success more impressive than a king-sized bed is a king-sized gymnasium.

112, 113. (Overleaf) In the late forties, Charles Eames designed and built this house from readily available industrial components, shipped to the site. He died in 1978. Ray, his wife and colleague, continues to preside over their design firm; last year in London she received on their joint behalf the Gold Medal of the Royal Institute of British Architects.

The house looks out over an empty meadow to the Pacific; one would never guess that a tumult of traffic pours continuously past the high hillside on which the house is built. One feels here in happy retreat from the exigencies of the world; the worn planks of the walkway urge us to pursue our just goals not in haste but as temperately as possible.

114. (Above) The Eames house was one of the so-called Case Study houses sponsored over a period of years by John Entenza, Editor of California Arts and Architecture Magazine. Designed by a variety of talented, venturesome architects, the houses did much to raise the aesthetic aspiration of homebuilders not only in Southern California but, indirectly, throughout the country as well. The Eames house is a pair of linked boxes, one of which is a residence, the other a studio.

115. (Opposite) The garden of the Irvin V. Willat house, in Hollywood, not far from Sunset Boulevard: a bungalow transformed into a "pueblo-Mediterranean" house.

116, 117. (Overleaf) Little has changed in the Willat house over the past half-century. (Willat himself died in 1976, at the age of eighty-six, and the house is still in the possession of his family.) When Willat remodeled the property, he was married to Billie Dove, a famous movie star, often described as one of the most beautiful women in the world. The Willats gave many glamorous parties in this house; among the frequent guests was Howard Hughes, whose movie company Billie Dove joined in 1929, after divorcing Willat. On the living-room wall is a likeness of Willat: a romantic and engaging visage. The room reflects the debonair catholicity of his taste, and so does the adjoining conservatory, which holds objects of art plucked from two or three centuries.

118. (Left) A nook that served once as a secular chapel honoring Billie Dove; above a Victorian chest of drawers, a rendering in stained-glass of the balcony scene from "Romeo and Juliet".

119. Irving J. Gill is an architect much admired by his fellow architects and almost wholly unknown to the general public. He makes no grand gestures; his presence is felt in the aptness and modesty of his designs.

The Miltimore house, pictured here, which pays silent tribute to the Spanish Colonial tradition in California by its use of arches, is characteristic of Gill in depending upon painted window trim for decoration. (The color of the trim – a curious dark blue-green – was of Gill's devising.) His residences reach out to embrace nature by means of porches and pergolas: spaces that provide shelter with the least possible sacrifice of light and air.

120, 121. The view from this hilltop estate reveals the intricate double nature of Los Angeles – its sunny urgency by day, its dreamlike implausibility by night. Though it is easy enough to believe that millions of people work hard in New York and London and Tokyo, we find it hard to believe that millions of people work hard in Los Angeles as well; the city strikes us as a fiction, superlatively well told, and on such a terrace as this we begin to remember Gatsby, a lifetime and a continent away. "In his blue gardens," Fitzgerald wrote, "men and girls came and went among the whisperings and the champagne and the stars." The aspirations of a Gatsby die early in the East, but who can be sure that they are not capable of being realized in the West? Isn't Gatsby's (and Fitzgerald's) error one of geography? Nothing is proposed in Southern California that cannot be made real.

116

122–124. No architect has shown a greater mastery of
the ranch-house style than Cliff May, who for over
forty years has been designing ranch-houses large and
small from coast to coast and even as far afield as
Ireland and Venezuela. His own ranch-house, though
within the city limits of Los Angeles, stands at the head
of a canyon seemingly untouched by man. At first
glance, the house resembles a village, with a scattering
of gabled roofs of different heights and with what might
be an ancient dove-cote rising out of them. The plan of
the house is by calculation so open that one is agreeably
unsure from one moment to the next whether one is just
entering a room or just leaving it. The main living-room
is large enough to embrace without crowding two
pianos, a portion of Mr and Mrs May's collection of
exotic musical instruments, and a stone fish (right).

125. (Overleaf) Generation after generation, century after century, the same complaint: what a pity it is that one can no longer command the quality of workmanship that was available in the past! The complaint was heard in the Renaissance and no doubt it was heard in Nineveh's prime as well, and it is never true; excellent workmanship, though rare, awaits only the taste and purse of a discriminating patron. This kingly sunporch is a case in point; its marble floor, mirrored walls, and furnishings are all of an unsurpassable elegance.

126. (Above) Frank Lloyd Wright designed the Sturgis house in 1939. He wished to demonstrate that a house could be designed on a low budget for "an ideal young married couple". The house occupies a steep site, to which it is tethered by a carport on the entrance side; most of the dwelling floats in space, cantilevered from a windowless brick base that contains the utilities. One is enabled to live outdoors by means of a long, south-facing terrace, onto which the living-room opens. Perhaps to save on the cost of lumber, the ceiling heights are exceptionally low, even for Wright. Mr Sturgis was a tall young man and is said to have practiced a constant ducking motion to prevent injuring himself as he made his way about the house. And then a Wrightian oversight: sooner or later, "an ideal young married couple" is likely to want children; when the Sturgises had a baby, the tightly organized little house proved too small for them and they were reluctantly obliged to move.

127, 128. Norma Talmadge was one of the leading stars of silent pictures. The large, shedlike building that was once her movie studio has been transformed into a sort of adult playhouse by the designer Tony Duquette. A variety of settings is hinted at, both indoors and outdoors: the old quarter of New Orleans, an English country house, a pavilion conjured up out of the Arabian Nights. Duquette's witty way with objects has given a bizarre concreteness to the metaphor of Hollywood as a dream factory.

129. (Left) In one corner of the dream factory, certain props have been arranged (or have diabolically arranged themselves) in such a fashion that they seem to be telling a story of some kind. Is that a loaf of bread on the console, or a human brain? Whose derby floats above the head of the young man in a perruke – a young man who may well be suggesting that we stroll elsewhere? The ravishing Chippendale side-chair is worthy of the ghost of Norma Talmadge, if only she will consent to put in a "cameo" appearance.

130. The basin is surely too heavy to be held up for long by these three hairy-legged fauns. The difficulty is for them to get out from under it without cracking their pates.

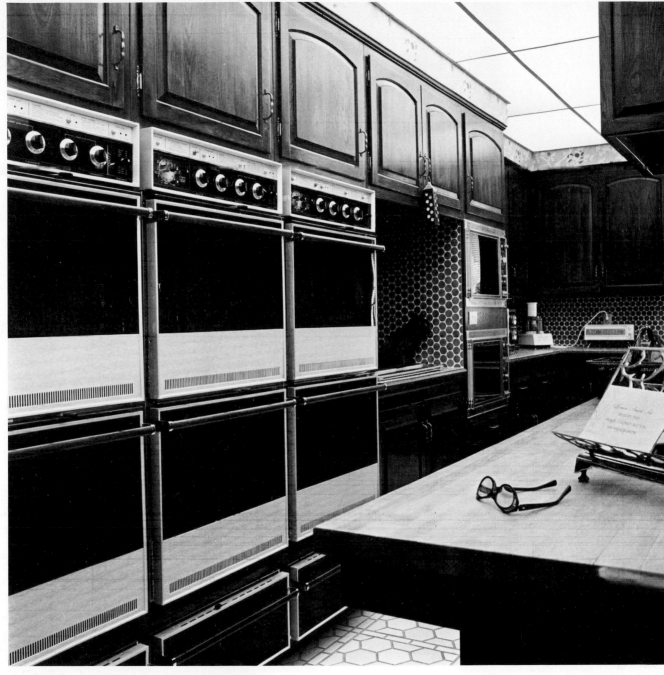

131–133. Diane Abramson is the most tireless of hostesses; in her big house she is happy to give sit-down dinners for a hundred or more guests. The Abramson kitchen boasts twenty-nine ovens – not a single oven too many. Mrs Abramson likes to cook and freeze innumerable dishes well in advance of their use, and she often names a special dish after a friend. A couple of immense walk-in freezers hold these dishes in readiness, all neatly wrapped and labeled.

In a lavatory at the Abramsons', a toilet of travertine, quarried not far from Hadrian's villa. Hadrian *redivivus* would find much to envy in the Abramsons' villa.

134, 135. Among the architects who gained early renown by his designs for Case Study houses is Pierre Koenig. The Beagles house, which Koenig designed in 1963, hangs above the Pacific Coast Highway like a nest in a treetop; one looks south over mile after mile of beaches to the far-off peninsula of Palos Verdes. The front of the house is an arrangement of glass screens facing a highway – a pleasant enigma, revealing nothing of its true nature. On the interior, the house unfolds around a stairway and fireplace; both are bigger than they need to be and so add a note of luxurious playfulness to an otherwise sternly disciplined design.

136. (Right) The garden side of a house designed by A. Quincy Jones. Water and cactus make up a contradiction so extreme as to make our eyes ache.

137–139. With his clients for this house A. Quincy Jones enjoyed that rare thing, an unbrokenly happy relationship throughout the long period of time that it takes to design and carry out a project. Having worked for many months over a set of plans that the clients at last pronounced satisfactory, Jones said, in effect, "All right, now that you've proved yourselves so understanding, why don't we try for something harder and better?" He then sat down and drew up a whole new set of plans, much bolder in concept than the first set (for which, as it later turned out, he refused to accept any payment). The house as built from the second set of plans gave pleasure equally to the clients and to Jones.

140, 141. Since the late forties, John Lautner has been hurling houses into existence in and around Los Angeles as if they were thunderbolts. Some inexpungeable residue of Frank Lloyd Wright can be found in Lautner, but he is, if anything, a greater melodramatist than the Master. His houses often contend with the adjacent terrain instead of accommodating to it, and in the case of the so-called "Chemosphere" house, built in 1960, Lautner abandons the terrain altogether. The house rests on the top of a mast, and although one can step out onto an improvised hillside terrace at one side of the house, the terrace is obviously an afterthought. Life is intended to be lived inside the capsule and what one sees through its windows is to be thought of as a view and has no other reality.

One of the pleasures of the "Chemosphere" house is the funicular railway that carries visitors up to the entrance. It asserts that we are stepping into a personal Disneyland and that we had better do so with a light heart.

142, 143. The "Chemosphere" house is a thickened frisbee, or perhaps a pumpkin pie with windows, and the plan provides more privacy than one might expect; there are three bedrooms and a couple of bathrooms, along with a big living- and dining-room and an adjoining kitchen.

In the master bedroom (above), contemporary necessities: a water-bed, a TV set, a telephone, a mirror, carpeted walls, and a few large potted plants.

144. On the heights above Silver Lake, Lautner has flung down a house as spectacular as its setting. Built in 1957, the house not only defies gravity but, in the case of a driveway that threatens to leap straight into the lake, spits in its face as well. Lautner likes to command an impertinent mingling of glass, stone, brick, and wood; a vast boulder that looks as if it had come to rest at some point in pre-history will turn out to have been a Lautner import of a few days earlier. Often enough, Lautner's houses have hidden away in them remarkable feats of engineering, by means of which a complex action is made to seem simple. In the Silver Lake house for example, an enormous picture window opens and closes in a motion that is simultaneously vertical and lateral.

145–147. The romance of the castle never dies. This late in the twentieth century and in no matter how unhistorical a form, we go on building our dreamed-of Camelots. The greatest castle ever erected along the Pacific is surely Hearst's San Simeon; the latest is this recently completed castle overlooking Malibu. Fierce as it may appear from a distance, mollifying civilities are to be discovered at close range, including a Jacussi countersunk into the stone floor of the terrace. There is also a large mirror built into a nearby wall (right), the purpose of which remains obscure. Perhaps it was intended to deceive marauders, who, mistaking their own reflected visages for those of a substantial garrison within, would thereupon beat a hasty retreat.

148. The front hall of the castle, constructed perhaps three-quarters of a century later than the house pictured opposite. To one's astonishment, the front halls have a few things in common: a grandfather clock, Oriental rugs, a stairway.

149. (Opposite) The architectural historian Robert Winter lives in this house, built and furnished in a style championed by the Craftsman movement, which flourished from the late nineties up through the First World War. Simplicity of means, simplicity of effect: it was an ideal radically at odds with the aspirations of millions of newly prosperous Americans, who were just beginning to taste the first fruits of conspicuous consumption. The castle at Malibu may be among the last of such fruits.

150–152. The movie director George Cukor has spent much of his long life in this house. It has been successfully added onto from time to time, and one wanders contentedly from room to room, never certain what the next doorway, the next turn of the stair, will reveal. Mr Cukor is a collector of pictures, books, and objects of art, which fill the house in controlled profusion; unlike some collectors, he has been careful not to be outmanoeuvered by his possessions. With one exception: a vine that is taking charge of the pavilion by his swimming pool and upon which, so Cukor says, he is afraid to turn his back as he goes by.

153, 154. (Overleaf) The exterior of the Cukor house may be said to be, though not very strictly, of the Regency period. One is put in mind of Brighton on a sunny afternoon; a holiday cheerfulness is in the air. Like so many of its neighbors, the house runs along the edge of a steep bluff, which Cukor has turned into a garden on half a dozen levels, circling up and around his bright-blue swimming pool. If the house could well be in England, the garden could be on the craggy heights of Capri, among wind-battered pines.

143

155. (Left) Memorabilia must be made room for, even if it
means crowding pictures onto the backs of doors. In a cubby-
hole of a study in a remote corner of the house, Cukor is
compiling a complete record of his career as a director. His
first movie, in 1932, was "Tarnished Lady", which starred
Tallulah Bankhead and had a screenplay by Donald Ogden
Stewart. His latest movie, made for television in 1978, was an
adaptation of Emlyn Williams's play, "The Corn Is Green", and
starred his old friend and favorite actress, Katharine Hepburn,
who appears in puppet form with Spencer Tracy in the gilded
proscenium that hangs between Colette above and Walter
Hampden below.

156. A stair-hall in the Cukor house is like a miniature
Guggenheim Museum; descending, one stops from moment to
moment to take in the drawings that fill every inch of wall. At
the head of the stairs, Cukor glances sidelong at Sargent's
celebrated charcoal of Ethel Barrymore.

157. (Above) When Mary Pickford and Douglas Fairbanks were at their happiest as mistress and master of Pickfair, their swimming pool was appropriately the grandest one in town. In those days, Pickfair appeared to be tucked away in a forest; now from the distant valley the Los Angeles of big business shoulders its way against the sky.

158. (Right) Before a stately house in Beverly Hills of approximately the same age and number of remodelings as Pickfair stands the obligatory white Rolls, without which making good in Hollywood is said to be but dust and ashes.

159. (Opposite) The drawing-room at Pickfair. Over the handsome mantelpiece is a portrait of Mary Pickford, which she never liked. While she was sitting for it, she was also trying to pass a kidney stone; the artist kept asking her to smile, and it wasn't easy.

160. (Left) In a basement room at Pickfair, a portion of
a large collection of paintings and photographs of Mary
Pickford. The lower of the two drawings to Pickford's
right is of her third husband, Buddy Rogers, who
survived her and who, having put Pickfair up for sale,
has been building a new house for himself a short
distance away.

161. (Above) An authentic nineteenth-century Western
bar, which Rogers inserted into a corner of the ample
Pickfair basement. The detailing of the bar is in the
neo-Renaissance style and the stained glass in the
cupboard doors is of high quality.

162. (Right) A lavatory at Pickfair.

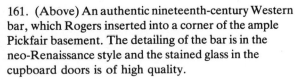

165. (Right) Allen Mink is a lawyer and a runner in marathons; Iris Mink is a child psychologist. Their swimming pool and pool-house were designed, like the main house, by Craig Ellwood. The symmetry of the pool-house (note how carefully the drinking fountain has been centered – what dread fate would have awaited the plumber if he had located it an inch to the left or right of center?) and the immaculate workmanship of the building are both characteristic of Ellwood. The flora on the hillside are also worth studying. The natural cover of the area is not forest but low bushes and grass; any big tree is sure to have been planted.

163. (Left) The Minks' hot-tub, which has become as necessary an appurtenance in Los Angeles today as a swimming pool used to be in the forties.

164. (Right) Mink's impressive assortment of running shoes; every pair represents a race that Mink has been a contestant in. Mink was born and raised in Brooklyn; it never occurred to him to become an athlete until he moved to California.

166–168. The Mink house is Ellwood's homage to Mies van der Rohe and his pioneering Farnsworth house. Philip Johnson paid Mies a similar tribute with his so-called "glass house" in New Canaan, Connecticut. The Johnson house is a plaything, consisting of a single large room for entertaining, a small bedroom, and a bathroom. The Mink house is on a much bigger scale; though it feels as light of heart as a weekend pavilion, it is a substantial and complex dwelling. Like the Farnsworth house (and unlike the Johnson house, which hugs the earth), the Mink house performs an uncanny act of levitation; it floats above a bed of black cobbles that give one the impression that a river of invisible water is constantly flowing over them. A side terrace (right) provides a clue to the size of the house. (Right, below) A view of the dining-room, with a painting by Ron Davis on the paneled end wall duplicitously pretending to be in three dimensions.

169, 170. Some of the floor-to-ceiling glass doors of the Mink house
slide open upon paved courts, where sunlight falls helter-skelter over the
green-gold leaves and mottled trunks of eucalyptus trees. Our eyes travel
back and forth through the trees, from wing to wing of the house; there is
no fixed point of vantage from which the composition of the whole is
intended to be viewed. In the dining-room, a sculpture by Fred Eversley;
in the living-room, a paradise of soft cushions and a carpet that looks
as if it might soon need mowing.

171–173. The twenties were the hey-day of make-believe in Southern California. Throughout the country, millionaires were building enormous Jacobean castles; in Los Angeles, people of moderate means but with the same fantasies were building diminutive Jacobean castles. (Above) Doorways far grander than need be have long been a commonplace in Los Angeles; however low the ceiling inside the house, the front porch is sure to be on a noble scale. Architects heightened the romantic nature of their houses by encouraging masons to trowel on stucco and plaster with a liberal hand (left); in the house to the right, stones are scattered, half-buried, over the surface of the building, like raisins in a rice pudding; two worried little eye-like windows peer out of what one guesses is a ground-floor lavatory, while another pair of eyes look down from a stunted steeple (perhaps once a chimney?) in the adjoining roof.

174–176. Not too much should be made of it, but a profusion of voluptuous curves is characteristic of the inanimate decoration of Hollywood. Examples worth noting are the mirror and sideboard at right, the fountain of conch shells below, and, on the opposite page, the tiles framing a Dutch "conversation piece" in one of several bars in the house of a local tycoon.

177, 178. The craftsmanship available to architects in Los Angeles half a century ago was of a surprisingly high order. Many follies were built, in a variety of styles – Norman, Swiss, Hawaiian – and they have proved unready to be demolished, the whimsicality of their design having little to do with the honesty of their construction. A favorite motif of the twenties was the rolled shingle roof (above), pretending to be thatch; few passers-by were deceived. (Opposite) The house of which this is evidently an imitation must have been three or four times its size. No matter – absurd as the reduced version is, it has been built with pride.

179, 180. Small as the bungalow at the upper left appears to be, it is, in fact, *two* bungalows. The desire to own one's house and land has always been so great in Los Angeles (and is so great today) that people will make any sacrifice of space to acquire them. A double house like this is divided straight down the middle, as accurately as if by a razor. Note that the crack in the sidewalk goes up the steps and across the porch, physically as well as symbolically splitting the house in two. The bungalow below, on the other hand, is one simple dwelling.

181. (Opposite) The yearning to move up in the world in aesthetic as well as financial terms is touchingly visible throughout the city. The grilles on the windows of this house imply that it may have begun life in a mildly Spanish vein; later, it went neo-Renaissance with a bang. The balustrade on the roof is so over-excited that its corner posts have outrun the house and hang in space.

182. (Above) In a semi-arid climate, gardening becomes an act of defiance, sometimes an obsession. Because Mary Pickford and Douglas Fairbanks were ardent Anglophiles, it was natural for them to add an old-fashioned English rose garden to the extensive plantings at Pickfair. In the twenties, the young Mountbattens spent a portion of their round-the-world honeymoon in the guest pavilion at the right. Out of respect, nothing has been altered in the pavilion since their time.

183. (Right) A successful evocation of Roman garden practices at George Cukor's house. The stone steps and walkways are in want of another century of wear.

184. (Opposite) The circular motor court of a large house by Wallace Neff, who used the turning radius of an automobile to establish the proper size of the court and who then (as Lutyens had earlier done in England) caused the shape of the house to follow exactly the curve of the court.

185, 186. (Opposite and right) Two views of a house that Cole Porter rented in the forties; it comes as close to being a conventionally pretty Long Island cottage as Porter was likely to find anywhere in California. Porter "adored" – as he would say – California and the assortment of singular individuals who had sprung up out of nowhere to take charge of the movie industry. When a song he wrote for the movie "Rosalie" – *In the Still of the Night* – made Louis B. Mayer weep, Porter was beside himself with pleasure; he held a high opinion of Mayer's aggressive nature. Mrs Porter failed to share her husband's delight in Hollywood society and soon abandoned it, but Porter stayed on; he relished the sunlight and the handsome young men who splashed in his pool as he lay in a deck-chair watching them. Gallantly, he continued writing songs that gave no hint of the constant pain he had endured since having been crippled by a fall from a horse many years earlier. His code called for him to be merry, and he did his best.

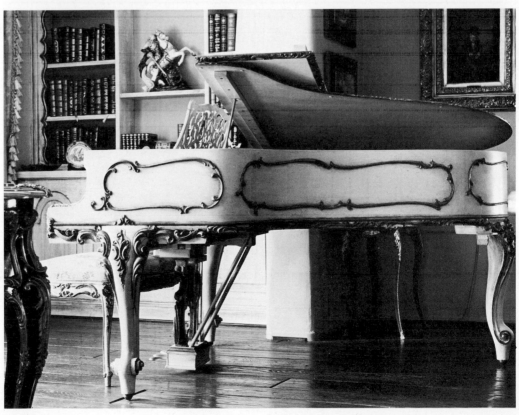

187. (Right) One of the few pianos of which it may be said with assurance that Porter never played it.

188. (Opposite) Like a diseased ghost of the Craftsman movement of long ago, a brutalist, make-shift, do-it-yourself style of architecture has gained a certain foothold in Los Angeles. People scour thrift shops, house-wreckers' yards, and even town dumps for treasures – a stained-glass window, a decorated tile, a piece of wood that, looked at from a certain angle, resembles a snake with two heads.

189. (Above) An antidote to the dishevelment of do-it-yourself architecture is this view of the pool at the Beverly Hills Hotel. How suavely in the light of afternoon is the waiter pouring a glass of spring water for the young woman coming without haste into her beauty!

190, 191. In the early thirties, the celebrated scene-designer for Metro-Goldwyn-Mayer, Cedric Gibbons, designed and built this house for his bride, the movie actress Dolores Del Rio. It is an admirable example of what was then generally known as *art moderne* and is now called *art déco*. Above, the walled tennis court, with an awninged pavilion for spectators; on the opposite page, the garden side of the house. At first glance, Gibbons appears to be employing the same vocabulary as Neutra and Abell, but we soon perceive that this is not the case; instead, he has produced a witty and highly romantic pastiche of what many of the foremost architects of the day were essaying in dead earnest. (An unexpected note of architectural "honesty" may be found in the downspouts, which leap from the coping of the roof without apology.) The scenery that Gibbons designed for M.G.M. when movies were at the height of their popularity influenced the taste of uncounted millions of Americans.

192, 193. Dolores Del Rio was an important movie star and no star can afford to be without a staircase that provides her with an ample amount of time in which to be admired as she descends it. Gibbons did well by his bride; this flight of stairs (left) is the primary element of design in the house. A secondary element is the use of mirrors. In the dining-room (above), we appear to be looking at a built-in sideboard with a bank of windows above it; actually, the windows are on the opposite side of the room and are being reflected in a long expanse of mirror. It was characteristic of the period to make use of as much built-in furniture as possible. The sideboard is one example; another is the couch and end table that fit below the landing of the stairs. Worthy of note is the practical black guard that keeps the edge of the table from being scuffed by vacuum-cleaners, floor-waxers, and the like. Also worthy of note is the adjacent air-vent, whose grille hints that it is going somewhere fast – an appearance of speed in stationary objects was a fad of the thirties.

194, 195. (Overleaf) On the left, the front door of the Gibbons house. The series of upside-down L's that form the architrave of the entranceway are charming, but why are they there? Similar L's, similarly without apparent function, decorate the flat stucco surface of the house. Right, a view of the living-room, with several favorite Gibbons devices on display: a built-in mirror, built-in furniture, and walls that give way, whether vertically or horizontally, as if out of politeness – "No, no!" they seem to protest. "You first!"

196–198. (Above) An interior view of the front entrance. At left, a mirrored toggle-plate in the Del Rio dressing-room, tactfully fitted to the wall with stars. (Opposite) Built-in lighting fixtures in the dressing-room. The relationship between an actress and mirrors has little to do with narcissism; she approaches the task of self-examination with dread, and it follows that a dressing-room is rarely a place for an actress to be happy in.

199. (Overleaf, left) A den in the house of the well-known author, Gore Vidal.

200. (Overleaf, right) An Egyptian disco/rumpus room in the house of Allan Carr, the movie producer.

201. (Left) The exterior of Mr Carr's pleasant Cotswold cottage gives no hint of the ancient, blood-red, King Tut-like wonders to be found in the disco room in his basement.

202. (Left) In Hollywood, not the least of the innumerable ways of measuring success is possession of a private screening-room. For a foxy mannequin poised on a chair-arm, add ten points.

203. (Opposite) Poverty is the friend of preservation and weathering is the friend of imitations. This pseudo-Spanish balcony is beginning to look more and more like the real thing.

204. (Above) The well-equipped dressing-room of Zsa Zsa Gabor. The wicker chair is for show; the folding chair is for getting down to business.

205. (Opposite) Miss Gabor seated on a bed that is very like a throne and deservedly so.

206–209. In Miss Gabor's wardrobe are
some shoes . . .

. . . and a few frocks as well.

The entrance to the Gabor kingdom.

A bar that plainly isn't intended to be sat at.

210. As Miss Gabor evidently knows, gardening in a hot climate is made easier by the use of plenty of big pots, tubs, and urns. Clumps of flowers in orderly profusion bloom the length of her vast, red-brick terrace.

211. At Cliff May's house, flowers in pots on a smaller scale flourish on both sides of an ancient Spanish grille.

212. Little by little over the past few years, a handful of nondescript houses has been turned into what one would swear was an ancient, blue-and-white village somewhere in the Netherlands. The gifted landlord rents apartments to actors, writers, and other people who have no need for permanent quarters in Hollywood. Peter Sellers recently occupied an apartment in the step-gabled building shown here.

213. John Lautner designed this swimming pool, in which water is made to run continuously over the far lip of the pool; one is convinced that the water is falling straight into Silver Lake – indeed, that the pool and Silver Lake are somehow miraculously one.

214. (Opposite) A nook in the make-believe Netherlands village. Here we are perhaps in a former Dutch colony, or in a make-believe former Dutch colony. Be that as it may, there is convenience to be found in close quarters: one leaps out of bed and into the nearby Jacussi with scarcely a pause for morning prayers.

215. (Above) A Churrigueresque entranceway and stairtower, carried out with skill and zest. Working in the Churrigueresque style, the architect who hesitates is lost.

216. (Overleaf, upper left) This one lost.

217. (Overleaf, lower left) A cottage once lived in by the composer-conductor John Philip Sousa; it has the look of drawing back apprehensively from its next-door neighbors.

218. (Overleaf, right) Formerly the house of the movie director Ernst Lubitsch. He had been in Mexico shooting a movie and, captivated by the native white-washed brickwork, he brought a crew of Mexican bricklayers back to Hollywood with him and put them to work. The bricks are oversize and the mortar is laid on in thick dollops. The handsome woman fresh from a swim is the present owner of the house.

219. (Left) Mrs Lion Feuchtwanger in the library of her house in Pacific Palisades. Widow of the well-known German novelist and bibliophile, she helped her husband to amass not one library but three. He lost his first library when the Nazis came to power and he and his wife were obliged to leave Germany and settle in France. He was engaged in collecting a second library when the Nazis swept over Europe in the Second World War; that library was lost. Moving to Southern California, the Feuchtwangers indomitably began to collect still a third library, which contains at present well over thirty thousand volumes. Mrs Feuchtwanger has already deeded the library to the University of Southern California.

220. (Above) The drawing-room of the Feuchtwanger house. There are books here and in every other room in the house except perhaps the kitchen. In a study upstairs is an ancient volume of Sophocles in Greek, annotated and signed by Michelangelo Buonarroti.

221. (Opposite) The entrance patio to the Feuchtwanger house. A large dark turtle is often to be seen padding about in this patio. He is a pet of Mrs Feuchtwanger's and follows her wherever she goes.

222, 223. In the house of the movie director Rouben Mamoulian, the cat pictured above is real and the monkey pictured below is not.

224. Rouben Mamoulian.

225. (Right) Still another Mamoulian cat.

190

226. The terrace of a house by A. Quincy Jones. Cliff May and Jones (who died in 1979) were old friends, and it is agreeable to see how well Jones, who had worked successfully in many other styles, carried off this bold and simple essay in the May ranch-house style. Not the least nervy thing about the house is how low Jones dared to bring the gable at both ends.

227. (Right) The main salon in Tony Duquette's adult playhouse. Henry James's family once teased him for being over-impressed by the amount of gold with which he had been surrounded during a weekend at a great English country house; James responded: "I can stand a good deal of gold." In the Duquette salon, one can stand a good deal of gold and brass and crystal and wire sunbursts and tapestried screens and Turkey-red rugs. One stares and is grateful.

228. In the nineteenth century, Herbert Spencer wrote, "Each of us begins to die when his organism becomes too puzzled to go on." Something like this seems to happen in the case of houses as well; they reach a point of deterioration at which it is useless any longer to dream of restoring them. The house above is surely just at that point: today it can be saved, tomorrow not. The rakish TV mast is a hopeful sign.

229. (Right) The artist Roman A. Clef and his friend, the critic Michael Leopold. They live in a studio of their own design, in an out-of-the-way quarter, and the world beats a path to their door.

230. (Left) Twilight in Beverly Hills. The implausible palms on their high trunks darken as the light fails, while the man-hole covers, so much lower than the palms, turn bright pink and gold.

231. An ordinary residence on an ordinary street alters its nature by the addition of an observatory. What can an amateur astronomer see of the heavens with the lights of Los Angeles blazing all round him? Perhaps it doesn't matter; perhaps he is content with the moon, such as it is.

232. The house above, with its solitary peg-leg, puts one in mind of mad Captain Ahab.

233. (Right) This house appears to have kept hoping to better itself by adding pillars and porches and balustrades, but in age the original house is emerging and may yet survive, four-square and without cosmetics.

234. (Opposite) What an ambitious turn-of-the-century house this was! If it cannot be saved, then the next best thing is to salvage as much of it as possible, for eventual display in some modest museum setting. It is sad when a house becomes an artifact, or a quarry for artifacts, but it is not as sad as when it vanishes without a trace.

235, 236. Two houses of unknown lineage, descended however indirectly from the Greene brothers but surely never seen by them. Houses of this simple and satisfactory design continue to stand by the hundreds and thousands throughout the city. They were built before air-conditioning and, being well-ventilated, can survive its loss.

237, 238. The lawns and gardens of Los Angeles have only to be regularly watered in order to produce a greenness rivaling Ireland's. Without water, the city would revert to a tawny scrubland, with scarcely a tree or a flowering shrub in sight. Meanwhile, the houses of the city grow ever more invisible. From one year to the next, hundreds of them are swallowed up by what amounts to an immaculate, carefully tended jungle; like ancient temples in Yucatán, they must be flown over to be found at all. Something like the same result is being accomplished within doors as well; it is often hard to tell whether one is in a drawing-room in Brentwood or in a rain-forest in Brazil.

239, 240. Peter de Bretteville's "high-tech" house is really a double house; one is occupied by de Bretteville and his family, the other by a tenant. The house gains dignity by its size, and something more than dignity; the eye takes pleasure in following the long line of windows and awnings that the two houses present to the sun. The de Bretteville house feels like some spare, exquisite ship from outer space, which has had the wit to beach itself on a California hillside. Already, it seems much at home there.

241, 242. Contrasting styles in contempory Los Angeles architecture: the house above gives us the reassurance that we count on when we follow principles of aesthetics that go back through time into pre-history: symmetry, repose, solidity, fitness for the purpose intended. The house on the opposite page, by Frank Gehry, is almost its opposite: unsymmetrical, on edge, flimsy, and giving no clue as to what it may be fit for – dare one even be sure that it is a house and not, say, a power station? And yet we find ourselves drawn to the Gehry . . . construction. We long to peer in at the windows and see how it works. Roughly, the choice in domestic architecture in the near future will probably be made between these two styles: a contest worth watching.

243. John Lautner has just finished an astounding house on the beach at Malibu. It leaps up out of the sand in a characteristically Lautnerian entanglement of wood, stone, steel, and glass, and then bends down as if to make obeisance to the sea. We observe that its roof is made of grass, and for no better reason than that Lautner thought it would be amusing to make it so. In a similar vein, the front door consists of a single large sheet of tempered glass, with no visible hardware. One simply presses with one's hand against the glass and the door swings open. We are entering Cloud-Cuckooland, and it appears likely that we will all be happy there.

Acknowledgements

Brendan Gill, Derry Moore, Christopher Phillips, and John Calmann and Cooper Ltd wish to express their gratitude to those who so kindly cooperated in the preparation of this book. Particular thanks are due to Dr Robert Winter, Esther McCoy, Randell Makinson, Michael Leopold and Roman A. Clef, who gave generously of help and advice.

Much-appreciated help also came from those listed below, as well as from many who prefer to remain anonymous.

Thornton M. Abell
Diane and Harry Abramson
April Antolini
Ron and Regine Atwater
Margaret and Danilo Bach
Patte Barham
Robert and Alice Beagles
Stephen Breimer

James Bridges
Gus Brown
Terry Brown
Phillip and Jacklyn Burchill
Allan Carr
John and Jeannie Carter
George Cukor
Peter and Sheila de Bretteville
Daniel Donohue
Tony and Beagle Duquette
Ray Eames
Astrid Ellersieck
Craig Ellwood
Mrs Lion Feuchtwanger
Ron Filson
Georges and Ann Fischer
Zsa Zsa Gabor
Katie Harp
Wendy Haymes
Thomas A. Heinz
Feliza Hertz
Margery and Max Hill
Baron Herbert Hischemoeller
Tom R. Hodges, M.D.
James Hoekema

Frank Israel
James A. Ito
Elaine Jones
Tina Kaye
Virginia Kazor
Kathy and Larry Keating
Tony and Kiki Kiser
Pierre Koenig
Jack Larson
John Lautner
Marion and Francis Lederer
Don Luckett
Rouben Mamoulian
A. Morgan Maree III
Cliff and Lisa May
Rosalind and Hal Millstone
Allen and Iris Mink
Maurice and Sue Faciano Mozur
Dion Neutra
William Markley Nixon III
Katherine Okie
Virginia and Gerald Oppenheimer
Constance Perkins
John R. Phillips
Paige Rense

Charles Buddy Rogers
Fredricka Saldivar
Vidal Sassoon
Sidney and Georgia Sheldon
Dian Spence
Betty Topper
Ramona Treffinger
Gore Vidal
Suzanne Vidor
Marjorie Walker
Mary Lou and Donald Wallens
Jeffie Pike
Eric Lloyd Wright
Betty Lou Young
Kelley Jeane Younger

Finally, the authors wish to
acknowledge the debt they owe to
John Calmann, whose tragic death
occurred just before the book went to
press, but whose energy and
enthusiasm motivated the whole
project.

Index

References in italic refer to plate numbers